# ALISON

On 17 August 1981, a pretty 19-year-old student, Alison MacDonald, set off on a short walk from the guest house at which she was staying in the Kashmiri village of Sonamarg in northern India. She never returned.

So what happened to the Aberdeen University judo enthusiast who, as a 14-year-old, wrote in a letter to a friend: 'I won't know what to do with my life unless the Lord takes me to India.'?

When her father, Kenny MacDonald, a 46-year-old trainee minister, arrived a few days later at Sonamarg, 8,000 feet up in the foothills of the Himalayas, he expected to discover that his daughter had fallen to her death in a ravine or perished in the fast flowing River Sindh.

Yet in spite of the biggest search ever mounted in the area, nothing was found, not even a scrap of clothing, and as time went by he became more and more convinced that his daughter, a devout Christian, had not met with an accident. Nor had she had a spiritual experience which caused her to close the door on her past.

That left just one other possibility – that she had been kidnapped. In a remarkable set of diaries kept during his eight visits to Kashmir, Kenny MacDonald records the events which led him to that conclusion: the secret meetings with the 'three musketeers' who said they could find her in return for the £6,000 reward; the allegations that she was abducted by soldiers; and the unexplained events in Sonamarg itself. They also reveal the courage, resourcefulness and, above all, the faith of a man who simply refused to give up.

In *Alison: A Father's Search For His Missing Daughter*, Quentin Macfarlane follows the remarkable story of one of the most intriguing and compelling mysteries of modern day.

# Alison

A FATHERS' SEARCH FOR HIS MISSING DAUGHTER

## QUENTIN MACFARLANE

MAINSTREAM
PUBLISHING

First published in 1986 by
MAINSTREAM PUBLISHING COMPANY (EDINBURGH) LTD
7 Albany Street
Edinburgh EH1 3UG


ISBN 1 85158 050 6   (cloth)
ISBN 1 85158 051 4   (paperback)

Typeset in Times by Pennart Typesetting (Edinburgh) Ltd
Printed in Great Britain by Billing & Sons Ltd, Worcester

For Rebecca.

# Acknowledgements

There are many people I wish to thank for their help in the writing of this book. One is my father, Alexander Macfarlane, for his constructive criticism and for pointing out some grammatical and spelling howlers! The others are those without whose co-operation my research would soon have foundered. Liz Merry is one of them. The events of August 1981 left her emotionally scarred, yet she recalled them for my benefit with great stoicism and courage. Her parents, Ian and Rosemary Merry, also provided invaluable information, pulling out fact after fact from the depths of their memories. Chrissie Kennedy, Betty Kelly, John Ray, Professor Donald MacLeod were among many other people, both here and in Kashmir, whose contributions were important in the piecing together of this story.

But most of all I want to thank Kenny and Reta MacDonald. Their hospitality and friendship during my many visits to their home in Rosskeen was warm and genuine. It must have been distressing for them to relive, in such vivid detail, their search for Alison but not once did it show. I've lost count of the hours we spent pouring over maps and documents and always they displayed the utmost patience – even when I repeatedly failed to grasp the order in which events occurred. Without Kenny's diaries this book would not have been possible. They record in great detail not only his efforts to find Alison but also his most private thoughts. I have tried to edit his diaries with discretion but I am only too well aware that my contribution was merely to reassemble what was already a remarkable and highly readable account of a man's search for his missing daughter.

I have been asked many times during the past year whether I think Alison is still alive. I don't know the answer to that, nor have I attempted to reach a conclusion in this book; I have left that for the reader. However the hope and faith shown by all the MacDonald family and many of their friends has been a joy to see and I can't deny that some of this has rubbed off on me. Many people, not just Kenny and Reta, are convinced that one day Alison will come home. I pray that they are right.

*Quentin Macfarlane*
*Aberdeen*
*July 1986.*

# Prologue

Young Grant Franklin felt terrible. Not only had he taken a bit of a ribbing from the other lads, he had also lost his camera. As he walked dejectedly back to the bus he was sorely tempted to say nothing in case the teasing started again. But his camera meant a lot to him so he asked the camp adjutant–'adjie' to the boys–whether he could go back to look for it.

"Of course," said Kenny, "I'll come with you. Where did you lose it, anyway?"

"Near the top," replied the gangling 12-year-old. "Me and some of the others were fooling around and they threw me in the heather. I think I must have lost it then."

They started running and within a matter of twenty minutes they were at the top of the 1,500-feet Fyrish Hill. Kenny, a very fit 46-year-old, was a popular figure at the Free Church summer camp at the nearby town of Dornoch and Grant felt rather pleased with himself at having kept up with the man who, all week, had shown that he hadn't lost any of his prowess on the football field.

Grant, the son of a doctor, was tall and skinny and simply didn't have the build for football. In fact, he wasn't very good at any sport, with the result that at school, and now at camp, he often felt left out of things.

But now he had proved that he could run, and run well and he felt a great sense of achievement. Kenny was also impressed by the youngster's pace over the grassy track and suggested he take up athletics.

Once they both recovered from the gruelling run, they started looking for the camera. By now it was obvious that Grant hadn't the foggiest idea where, in the vast expanse of heather, he had been shoved so they decided to start at the top and work their way down. They knew roughly which route to take from their position in relation to the curious monument which overlooks the village of Evanton below.

The distinctive landmark on the summit of Fyrish Hill was erected by Sir Hector Monro of Novar, who lived from 1726–1805.

As a General in the British Army he gave distinguished service in India and, on his return, decided to build a monument to provide work for local unemployed men. The monument, he decreed, would be a replica of the gates of Negapatam, the scene of one of his greatest victories. Hence an unlikely link had been established between India and Easter Ross in the Scottish Highlands.

After searching, without success, for 10 or 15 minutes, Kenny suggested they pray together. As a trainee minister he had no difficulty in finding the right words.

"Lord, help us to find Grant's camera. But if it is not to be found, help to cushion the disappointment for him."

As they opened their eyes, the camera was lying almost at their feet. Grant's relief was matched only by Kenny's incredulity.

They had stopped at that particular place purely by chance; indeed Grant had said he thought his fall had *not* happened there. Yet, there the camera lay in full view of both of them.

As they quickly scrambled down the hill to the waiting bus, Kenny tried hard not to let the youngster see how much the incident had affected him. So far as he was concerned this was a clear, unambiguous, example of a prayer being answered. He had never doubted the power of prayer but at no time in the past had it manifested itself so dramatically and so instantly. What better way, he thought, of letting young Grant see how the hand of God guided those who believed in Him.

What Kenny didn't know was that in two months time he would again be praying on the top of a hill, not for the return of a camera but for the return of his missing daughter, Alison. The association between Fyrish Hill and India had been well documented in local history books but his association with that country was only just beginning.

# 1

I first became involved in the Alison MacDonald case in the last week of August 1981. At the time I was news editor of Northsound, the Aberdeen-based independent radio station and, as Alison was a student at Aberdeen University, the story of her disappearance featured prominently in our news bulletins.

Journalists who came in contact with the girl's father, Kenneth MacDonald, over the following two or three years couldn't help but be impressed by the tenacity and resourcefulness of this former customs officer. His conviction that his daughter was still alive burned in him so deeply that it affected many of those in whom he confided. His wife, Reta, remained quietly in the background as he shuttled back and forth to Kashmir in his search for Alison but later, as I got to know them, I realised that she was a major source of strength and encouragement.

Alison disappeared on 17 August 1981 while on holiday with a university friend, Elisabeth Merry. One morning she left the guest house in which they were staying, bought three apples at a fruit stall across the road, and never returned.

Kenneth MacDonald's frequent trips to India to follow up fresh leads kept the story in the news. But as time went by there seemed little hope of finding the girl alive and the MacDonalds were probably regarded by most people as a family who could not or would not face up to the truth.

Kenneth MacDonald – Kenny to everyone who knew him – was studying to be a minister at the College of the Free Church of Scotland in Edinburgh, having given up his career in H.M. Customs and Excise. He had not yet completed the first year of a four-year course when Alison disappeared. There were those who came in contact with him who admired the handsome former amateur international footballer for his remarkable cheerfulness in the face of such intense personal sadness and disappointment. They felt that he seemed to keep going by a combination of his unfaltering Christian faith and a growing belief, based on information he had received abroad, that Alison had been abducted and was still alive.

11

Hard-nosed journalists were naturally sceptical of his claims. Alison had, after all, gone missing in a mountainous area close to the Pakistan and Chinese borders and teeming with soldiers of the Indian Army, most of whom hadn't had contact with a woman for months – certainly not with a pretty 19-year-old European girl. Quite apart from the risk of being raped and killed by sex-starved soldiers there were also the natural dangers of this spectacularly beautiful region; wild animals that inhabit the snow-capped mountains and fast-flowing rivers whose milky blue glacial waters would surely crush to death against the jagged rocks anyone unfortunate enough to fall in.

Kenny MacDonald wisely didn't tell the news media everything. In fact he was an adroit manipulator of the press, using it when he needed publicity, keeping quiet when news coverage might have jeopardised delicate negotiations. The man who had the job of keeping reporters at bay was his mentor and friend, Professor Donald MacLeod of Free Church College.

I had an idea there was more to this case than Kenny MacDonald had ever revealed publicly and in the summer of 1985 I wrote to him at Invergordon, where he was now minister of Rosskeen Free Church, to ask whether he would co-operate with me in the book I hoped to write about his continuing search for Alison. A few days later he phoned me and we fixed a date for a meeting.

Free Church Manse, Rosskeen, is a modern, detached house with a long, sloping front garden and a battered old caravan at the back. It is situated at the top of a hill overlooking the church and from Kenny MacDonald's study window there's a clear view of the Cromarty Firth. The MacDonald's home is comfortably, if economically, furnished and you get the impression that life on a Customs officer's salary and later a minister's stipend, has taught them to make the most of things. There are a few examples of Kashmiri craftwork brought back by Reta from her two visits there and a map pinned to the wall of Kenny's study has several crosses in ink showing villages in Kashmir and Pakistan to which he has been in his search for Alison.

I told him I did not plan to carry out my own investigation into what happened to her: my purpose was to write about the extraordinary lengths to which he had gone to find her. He, after all, had visited Kashmir eight times since Alison disappeared, spending a total of six months there. It was therefore unlikely that I or anyone else could uncover any significant new facts. He agreed to be interviewed, adding: "You never know you might just come up with something I overlooked or regarded as unimportant at the time."

The trail had gone cold over the preceding 18 months and I was left with the distinct impression that he was prepared to confide in me in the slim hope that my inquiries might give the investigation much-needed new impetus. But I don't think he considered that a strong possibility; nor did I.

Kenneth MacKinnon MacDonald was born in the village of Skinidin on the Isle of Skye on 9 January 1935. He had two older brothers and five sisters and the family was completed by two cousins who were raised with them. His father was a general merchant cum crofter and his mother had enough to do rearing and looking after ten children.

"It was a big, happy family," he recalled. "We had family worship night and morning and all decisions were made on Scriptural grounds. But I don't want to give the impression of a strict upbringing. It was a very happy, carefree home life within the bounds of Christianity."

He went to primary school in the nearby village of Colbost and at the age of 11 he moved to another school at Dunvegan where he remained for four years. Then it was off to the senior secondary on the island's only town, Portree, where, during term, he lived in a hostel. He left school at 18.

"I suppose I was bright enough, but I was never a scholar. My mother used to say that 'I never took my brain out of the polythenc bag.' I read books, mostly adventure stories but as regards book work for learning, no I never did that."

I asked him if he had any particular memories from his school days.

"We had a teacher in primary school with a big, gold watch which we went in and out by. So one day when she was out at dinner I sneaked into the class and put the watch three quarters of an hour ahead, with the result that instead of getting out at the usual time of four, we actually got home at quarter past three. So we all got away three-quarters of an hour early which I thought was a tremendous success but, of course, I got the belt the next morning.

"Another thing I remember was when I was at the Portree school where I had the dubious distinction of being expelled two days before the end of term. It was really funny.

"It was the time of the local Mod and some of the senior boys were acting as ushers and taking money at the door. Two or three of my mates took too much to drink because one of their friends had won the gold medal so they all got slightly oiled. Unfortunately they were seen by a schoolmaster and the following day they were told to go home, even though there were only three days left till the end of term.

"It so happened that one of the lads had to go all the way to the outer isles and there was a boat leaving that night. Then I remembered that there would be another boat leaving Portree in a couple of days time to take the rest of the pupils home so I said to this boy: 'Don't bother going home tonight. Go to my home in Skinidin, wait there for two days and then catch the boat as though nothing had happened.' Unfortunately the headmaster phoned the parents to say their boy was on his way home, so when he didn't arrive they phoned the police and there was a tremendous hue and cry until they found him back at Skinidin happily painting the gates of my parents' home. So as soon as the headmaster heard about that, I was locked in a room and wasn't let out until my mother and father came to take me home."

"As a youngster were you good at sport?"

"I used to be very keen on running. Sometimes I felt as though I could run for days without getting tired. My father had sheep and cattle and we were always getting in the hay – there weren't tractors in those days. It was all done by hand and we had sheep on an island so we did a lot of boat work. There was always something to be done."

"Did you ever have the urge to leave the island for the bright lights of, say, Glasgow?"

"No, I found life was absolutely full because there were so many things going on. We used to arrange football and shinty matches and go to dances and things like that. It was a tremendous

14

existence and ideal for kids growing up. We had to cycle four or five miles to get to the nearest entertainment. I never left Skye at all – there was no need to."

It was in Glasgow, in 1957, after National Service, that Kenny began a career in H.M. Customs and Excise that was to span nearly quarter of a century. At school he'd been good at football but now, at the age of 22, he was on the verge of a career in the professional ranks. "When I was in Glasgow I played for St Johnstone and then moved to England and played for some of the top amateur sides. It was while I was there that I was approached by Spurs."

The invitation to join one of Britain's most illustrious football clubs came from no less a person than the manager of the time, Billy Nicholson. Kenny had been spotted while playing for Scotland's amateur side against Wales and he met Nicholson at Heathrow Airport when the Tottenham manager was on his way with his side to a match in Europe. By this time Kenny, now a Customs officer at Heathrow, was 24 and he reckoned it was a bit too late in life to give up a good job for the unpredictable world of professional football.

"I remember one time when I was down in London a story appeared in one of the daily papers that I was from a croft in Skye. Not long afterwards, during a bad game, I heard a section of the crowd shouting: 'Awa hame to yer croft, MacDonald.' I think I just laughed it off."

In 1958 Kenny had married Reta Cromarty whom he had met in Elgin while doing his National Service. She was born in Orkney on 1 December 1937; her father was a stonemason and the family – she had a brother and sister – lived in the small fishing village of St Margaret's Hope, south of Kirkwall. When she met Kenny she was 16 and attending a pre-nursing college and they were married five years later at Ashford in Middlesex. Kenny and Reta MacDonald's first child, Mairi, was born in London in 1960. And on Christmas Day the following year Reta gave birth to their second daughter, Alison Ishbel, at the family home at 152 Clare Road, Stanwell, Staines, Middlesex. Only fourteen months separated the two girls and they were to develop a deep, lasting friendship.

The first of the MacDonald boys, Sam, was born in Aberdeen in 1964. Kenny's job had taken him there two years earlier and they lived in a rented house at Blairs on the South Deeside Road. However they were soon back in London where Kenny had been promoted to the rank of preventive officer at Heathrow. Then, in 1967, they uprooted themselves again, this time for Lewis, the largest of the Outer Hebridean islands. The main town on Lewis, in fact the only town, is Stornoway where on Saturday nights the pubs are full of islanders getting a few last drams in before the Sabbath. Knowing what the Free Church's attitude was to alcohol, I wondered whether Kenny enjoyed an occasional drink.

"Not really. I was never very fond of drinking or smoking so I never had these temptations. But at home I still like a glass of wine or a dram. I've no strong views about it."

I wanted to know if, in Lewis, religion was an important part of his life. "Yes, towards the end of our stay there it was because I understood more and more about the Bible and the word of God and it was important I used what little time I had left there to tell other people about Christ. I am tremendously fond of people and in the Customs I met thousands upon thousands of people of all different nationalities and I got very fond of them, so I felt I had to tell people about Christ.

"I had always known that I would come to a knowledge of the good things of life – that the lord Jesus was my saviour. And in Lewis I came to understand this in a more intimate way and from then on it began niggling me that I should be doing something for the Lord other than just eating my own bread and butter.

"I could tell others about the Lord and it was the fact that I had so many lovely friends who were tremendous people and yet they were going on from day to day without any knowledge of the Lord; without any knowledge that one day everything was going to come to an end.

"Looking back on my life I'm firmly convinced that the seeds of Christianity were sown by my parents. Two things – my mother's teaching and my father's example – never left me and I knew what was right from then on."

In Lewis the MacDonalds lived in Coll, a village seven miles from Stornoway. Home was a smallholding around which a few sheep and cattle grazed. Mairi and Alison both went to the local primary school in the district of Back but according to their mother they spoke with an accent "more English than Scots". They had, after all, begun their school life in Middlesex; at St Anne's Primary, Stanwell. Unlike their father, a native Gaelic speaker, neither could get too excited about the Celtic tongue.

The second of the boys, Derek, was born on 13 January 1969 by which time Alison was seven. It was a happy, carefee upbringing and as they got older the children had to learn some of the essentials of island life like cutting peat and helping out during lambing.

Religion was important to the MacDonalds as it is to many people in the Western Isles where the Free Church and Free Presbyterian Church have little difficulty in finding supporters for their uncompromising brand of Protestantism. At home the Gospel was an important part of the children's daily lives in what Kenny described as "an essentially loving fashion". I wanted to know at what point he decided to give up the security of his job for the frugal and precarious existence of a trainee minister. He wasn't sure exactly but felt that an experience of Alison's when she was 13 may have been a contributory factor.

In the summer of 1975 Alison went off to Free Church camp at Avoch on the Black Isle, a part of Inverness-shire which, although surrounded by water on three sides, is as much an island as Cornwall. There she met someone who had a deep influence on her. Miss Isabel MacIver was the camp commandant or 'commie' as she was affectionately known by her young charges, and under her guidance Alison's life changed. She became a committed Christian and in a letter the following year to Nina MacPherson, another girl at the camp, she wrote: "I feel I won't know what to do with my life unless the Lord takes me to India."

I wanted to know whether the MacDonalds had found it difficult to abandon their contented way of life in Lewis for the sacrifices they would have to make in Edinburgh. By this point in the interview Reta had joined us.

Kenny said: "Everything became subservient to the fact that I was going into the ministry. I think Reta had the biggest turmoil in her life because in Lewis we had sheep and cattle, hens, ducks, dogs and cats and she had to change her whole way of life. I knew what I was letting myself in for. There would be about sixty exams and a lot of hard self-discipline and study. But once you've set your mind to it, you've no regrets, you just knuckle down and get on with it. And I think I became a much better scholar than when I was a teenager."

"How difficult was it academically?"

"Not as difficult as I thought. I suppose I did enjoy the study part of it to a certain extent. But the course was interrupted by Alison being lost so I only spent a year there when I was wholeheartedly wrapped up in my studies."

Occasionally, Reta would chip in to agree with her husband or to add some small detail he had left out. Her slim figure and straight, blonde hair made her look younger and as she sat, cross-legged on a chair, it occurred to me that she wouldn't have looked out of place at a beatniks' reunion. She produced mugs of coffee and a plateful of home-made scones and we talked about Mairi and Alison. What were they like as children, I asked.

"They fought a lot but they were great friends. I don't know if we ever spoke about them singly, it was always Mairi and Alison. They were always together and they ganged up on Sam a bit. They started school in London and then we moved up to Lewis so they had a free lifestyle there, running wild on the croft. It was a nice childhood, very free and easy."

"Was Alison good at her school work?"

"She was the brightest in the family and she did very well in her exams without having to try too hard. She was the only one of us who liked to read Dickens and things like that."

At school, Alison's best friend was Chrissie Kennedy, a bonny Gaelic-speaking girl from the same village. They became chums in their first year together at Back Primary and by the time they were old enough to go to the Nicolson Institute in Stornoway, the islands' senior secondary school, they were inseparable. They shared their secrets and dreams and when Alison used to drum her fingers on a school radiator as though it were a piano only Chrissie knew she was mimicking Freddie Mercury of the rock band Queen.

Alison, never as slim as her sister, had the wholesome good looks of a girl brought up in the country. But how she wished she didn't have those rosy cheeks that made her look as though she had just stepped out of *Brigadoon* or *The White Heather Club*.

At the Nicolson she was one of the school's most able pupils. She got 'A' grades at Higher level in English, History, French and German and by the time she was in her sixth year there, the school could offer her no more academic challenges. One day, four weeks into the start of her final year, she arrived home and told her parents: "I'm bored, I'm not going back." The following day the headmaster phoned Aberdeen University and asked if they had a place for a late applicant with good Highers. A few weeks later she was on her way to Aberdeen.

Alison was still only 17 but although very much a home-loving girl, she adapted well to her new environment. The main subjects in her Master of Arts degree course were history and religious studies but she didn't have to work too hard to keep up and found plenty of time for other things.

She'd always been good at sport. At school she was a keen netball player but at university her attention turned to judo. Soon she found herself in the university team and was considered by her tutor, Dr Colin Pearson, a biology lecturer, to be "a very good beginner". Good enough, in fact, to get her green belt after less than a year.

Sometimes she was asked to take part in a match on a Sunday but always declined. She didn't make a fuss about it and few of her team mates knew the reason: like a more famous athlete before her, Eric Liddell, she believed participating in sport on a Sunday to be a sin. Later, in India, her insistence on observing the Sabbath was to play a significant part in her disappearance.

"She also did ballroom dancing which we always thought funny," said Reta. "But I think a lot of the judo people did ballroom dancing. She was also in the university's Task Force team. On Saturdays she cleaned out a Cyrenians' shelter for alcoholics which must have been grim, and on Wednesday afternoons she helped with a children's playgroup at Powis. She gets on very well with children, particularly younger children. She was great pals with Derek who was so much younger than she was."

I wanted to know more about Alison's religious views, particularly her experience at Free Church camp when she was 13. What effect, I asked Reta, did this have on other members of the family? "I think it happened at a time when all of us were thinking more positively about religion. Maybe we weren't

19

aware of it at the time but I think we were all searching for a faith or something. We all realised it was something good that had happened to Alison."

"How did she change?"

"I think she became more tolerant towards us and she started thinking more about doing things for others. She was setting her life out to serve Jesus rather than seeking personal ambition or whatever thoughts she had before."

"Would you describe her as a loving daughter?"

"Yes, very, very. We were always great friends. The whole family are close. I suppose that's why we miss her."

"Did she talk about what she wanted to do when she left university?"

"I don't think she really had much idea what she wanted to do. She did history and religious studies but I don't know that she thought these would be significant in what she was going to do."

"Did she talk about going to the Third World?"

"Yes, we probably felt it would be very like her to do that. I think that had she decided to do missionary work we would all have been thrilled. What she would have done with a history degree, though, I don't know!"

"Do you think she may eventually have become a missionary?"

"No, but I think she was very interested in this. She was very interested in India."

Reta then recalled the letter Alison, as a fourteen-year-old, had sent to her friend Nina MacPherson.

"It was only recently when Nina was sorting out letters that she discovered this letter from Alison sent all those years ago. She came to the bit about Alison not knowing what to do with her life unless the Lord took her to India and I think she felt a bit sort of prickly when she read it."


It was through the judo club that Alison met Liz Merry, the girl she was later to go to India with. Liz, the older of the two by 20 months, also enjoyed the outdoor life and they decided to spend part of the forthcoming summer holidays grouse beating at Tomatin near Inverness. Liz was studying medicine and she knew already she would be going to India in four years time as an elective student, possibly to work in a leper colony. So as they tramped through the heather and bracken together seeking out game for the advancing guns, they came up with the idea of saving up to go to India the following summer. At that point it was nothing more than an interesting possibility and it was several months before they got down to discussing it seriously.

The holiday at Tomatin lasted a month and when Alison returned to Aberdeen to start her second year she was joined by her friend, Chrissie Kennedy, who had come over from Lewis to start a degree course in Celtic studies. Their friendship was as strong as ever. They would go to the cinema two or even three times a week and they saw *Dogs of War*, the thriller based on the Frederick Forsyth novel, no fewer than four times. Chrissie knew the film so well she could recite much of the dialogue.

After the first term they moved into digs at 164 Deeside Gardens, the home of Gordon and Hilary Paterson and their three young children. Deeside Gardens is a long loop of houses off Great Western Road and the Paterson's semi-detached home is roomy and comfortable.

The girls shared a bedroom and had the run of the kitchen providing Mrs Paterson, a stout, cheerful woman in her late thirties, wasn't using it. The Patersons, members of the Plymouth Brethren religious sect, enjoyed the girls' company and sometimes asked them to join the family for Sunday lunch.

Behind the Paterson's home in Aberdeen is the old Deeside Railway. The rails have long since been lifted and the disused line is now popular with ramblers and dog walkers. The railway, which began in 1853, went through some of Scotland's finest scenery and when the line was extended to Ballater thirteen years later, trainloads of day trippers would leave Aberdeen's Joint Station to enjoy the view. But the popularity of the motor car sounded the death knell for many small uneconomic lines and on 30 December 1966 a Class B1 locomotive – 61180 – hauled the famous railway's last train. Alison and Chrissie often wandered along the grassy track and daydreamed. They talked about getting married, and although neither had ever had a long-lasting relationship with a boy they loved the idea of family life.

And they fantasised a little. At Cults, one of Aberdeen's smartest suburbs, big, detached villas look down over the railway and Alison would imagine aloud that she lived in one and owned a white Jaguar XJ6. She loved the style of the 1930s and 1940s and a picture of Fred Astaire looked down on her from the girls' bedroom in Deeside Gardens. Once she splashed out £57 of her meagre student grant on a silk dress that suddenly took her fancy. She wore it only once.

I asked her mother whether she ever had boyfriends. "She had boyfriends," said Reta, "but nobody she was obviously very interested in. But we met a few from Aberdeen. Off and on there were young lads who came past the house in Lewis when she was about 12 – much to her father's horror."

"Would you describe her as pretty?"

"Yes, no, no not exactly pretty. Nice looking but she had rosy cheeks which were always a horror to her and she's plumper than Mairi, but with nice curly hair. She got on well with people. She was very much a tomboy. She was always friends with boys through school and got on well with them when she was growing up."

"Did she want to get married and have kids?"

"Oh yes, she loved kids and I think it would have happened. I just think she hadn't met anyone who appealed to her. But she certainly wouldn't have thought no, this isn't for me."

## 2

A few months after their grouse-beating holiday at Tomatin, Alison and Liz met in the street in Aberdeen. "Do you fancy hitch-hiking to India?" asked Liz. "Yes, when are you leaving?" came the reply. Liz wasn't serious about hitch-hiking but Alison's instant response appealed to her sense of the ridiculous and the two girls then started working on a more practical plan for getting to India. The air fare was the biggest expense. Alison paid for hers out of her grant and with money from her father. Strictly speaking it was really a loan but, without saying so, he had intended it to be a gift.

During the Easter holidays Alison returned to Stornoway to earn enough to live on during the six to eight weeks they would be away. She worked in Mathieson's supermarket filling shelves and by the time she and Liz flew out from London on 28 July 1981 she had saved just under £200. Clearly they wouldn't be staying in the best hotels.

On the day they left the crowds in London were already seeking the best vantage points for the wedding of Prince Charles and Princess Diana the following day. The two girls met at the airport. Alison arrived with a girlfriend at whose home, near Heathrow, she had spent the night. Liz and her father drove there from the family home in Hampshire.

Thai Airlines flight TG911 left on schedule at 10.10 a.m. and arrived in Delhi at 1 a.m. the following morning. The girls enjoyed the trip. The attractive hostesses wore long, silk dresses which Liz assumed were their national costume and she thought the orchids and hot scented towels given to passengers was a nice touch.

Both girls intended to keep diaries of their holiday and in hers Liz recorded their first minor setback in India. 'Taxi to hotel near railway with en suite hole! Awoke noon. Took rickshaw to new hotel.'

They were luckier next time. The Hotel Vishal was marginally less basic and they used this as their base for touring the city.

Years of exposure to the scorching summer heat has taken its toll on the many fine buildings erected by Sir Edwin Lutyens when he was commissioned in 1911 to design India's new capital. The heat and the dust combine to make the atmosphere oppressive and high above the city a yellow film of industrial pollution acts as a filter against the sun's rays. Yet New Delhi has as many parks and open spaces as most of Europe's capitals and the imperial grandeur of its monuments and Government buildings give it a prosperous, even opulent appearance which contrasts, sharply, with the unremitting poverty of the old city and the shanty towns nearby.

The girls saw India Gate, the 42-metre-high arch raised in memory of the 90,000 soldiers of the Indian Army who died during World War 1. They visited Humayun's Tomb, a sort of prototype of the Taj Mahal and at the Red Fort they watched a spectacular son-et-lumiere kaleidoscope of India's past from the Mogul emperors to the British.

They also did more mundane things like trying out the loo at the Oberoi Intercontinental and bingeing on sweet Indian cakes; Liz had a pair of trousers made.

When they left home the only place they were committed to visiting was a leprosy hospital. For Liz this was important and Alison was quite happy to go along with her friend's idea. In Delhi, they made arrangements to spend two weeks at a hospital in Nepal towards the end of their holiday and that meant getting a visa for the small Himalayan kingdom.

On the Saturday they sought out a church to attend the following day. In her diary, under Sunday 2 August, Liz wrote: 'Returned to Kosla cafe for toast breakfast in spite of being a little sick previous night. Did washing. Walked to Sikh temple and then to Free Church of North India. All denominations, very friendly. Met Glaswegian in church and had tea after service.'

The following day they left the Hotel Vishal at 6 a.m. to catch the train to Agra. Alison, particularly, wanted to go there to see the Taj Mahal and they found themselves sharing the train with holy men on their way to a religious festival.

According to the girls' diaries the Taj Mahal was 'phenomenal' and 'magnificent' and both felt it worth recording that the same day they saw the burning funeral pyre of a Hindu soldier.

The next day, 4 August, they visited Agra's Red Fort, a smaller but no less impressive version of the one in Delhi and later they were invited to tea in a nearby house. In her diary

Liz noted that earlier in the day they 'had some trouble with boys'. By this time they had decided to travel north to Kashmir. They looked at the map and thought, mistakenly, they could cross the border into Nepal that way. So they left Agra for the arduous journey to Srinagar, the summer capital of Kashmir. After 14 hours on a train, travelling third class, they arrived at the city of Jammu, some 180 miles south of their destination.

In Jammu they were invited out for a drink. In her diary, Alison wrote: 'Met a man in a cafe – again at 7.30. Taken to hotel. Beer, sandwiches.' Liz also recorded the event: 'Arrived Jammu 3 p.m. Hotel Diamond. Then met enginering factory owner and were treated to cold beer, a real luxury (cheapest Rs 8)'. What they didn't write down was the fact that the man made suggestive remarks to them and, according to Liz, seemed to be particularly interested in Alison.

In his Booker Prize winning novel, *Midnight's Children*, Salman Rushdie eloquently describes the Kashmir valley and the city of Srinagar in which Alison and Liz had now arrived.

In those days the radio mast had not been built and the temple of Sankara Acharya, a little black blister on a khaki hill, still dominated the streets and lake of Srinagar. In those days there was no army camp at the lakeside, no endless snakes of camouflaged trucks and jeeps clogged the narrow mountain roads . . .

The valley lics to the north of the state of Jammu & Kashmir and from the high Himalayan peaks that provide such a dramatic backdrop, glacial streams make it a fertile and green contrast to the dry and torrid plains to the south.

In spring, the valley awakens from the harsh winter that swiftly erases memories of the warm, sultry summer, and on the lower slopes the sycamores and birches shake off the last of the melting snow. On the Dal Lake pied kingfishers dive for their silvery prey like meteorites falling from the sky and high in the mountains an occasional solitary golden eagle soars.

In summer the gently sloping meadows are a carpet of forget-me-nots and snowdrops and, on the lake, the pink-red flowers of the lotus plants dance a watery dance in the still air. Honey bees seek out the apple blossom and saffron and in the paddy fields women and children tend to next year's harvest.

Jammu & Kashmir has four and a half million inhabitants and it is India's most northerly state. It is bordered on the north and east by China and to the west by Pakistan. The state's strategic importance has left it vulnerable to hostile neighbours and more than a third of Kashmir is now part of Pakistan. A smaller slice, in the east, is in Chinese hands.

Politically, it is a sensitive area and border disputes are common. There is a large military presence but many of the mainly Muslim Kashmiris regard the Indian Army as an army of occupation and would rather see Kashmir totally independent of India or part of Islamic Pakistan.

It was against this background that Alison MacDonald and Liz Merry arrived in Srinagar on Friday 7 August 1981 after a bumpy and, at times, hair-raising 12-hour bus journey from Jammu. Like most tourists who come to this city of just under half a million people they made for the houseboats that line the floating gardens of the Dal Lake like row after row of beached Noah's Arks. Oddly, the houseboats of Srinagar are a British creation. During the Raj, the sahibs and memsahibs of imperial Britain sought respite from the searing heat of Calcutta and Bombay in the cooler temperatures of Kashmir. There, they tried to build summer homes and hunting lodges but when the then Maharaja refused permission, they neatly sidestepped the no-building ban by setting up home on the water. Thus, the houseboats came into being and to this day they are designed and furnished in the sumptuous manner to which their original occupants were accustomed.

The usual way of reaching the houseboats is by shikari, a long, narrow timber boat rather like a canoe. Some have gaily painted canopies draped with gaudy tassels and fabrics to shield against the sun. The boats have exotic names like *Golden Valley* or *Snow Queen* and a board nailed to the fore end of the canopy boasts 'deluxe comfort' or 'full spring seats' into which the unsuspecting passenger sinks like a sack of potatoes.

Many of the shikaris leave from jetties or ghats off the Boulevard, a busy, tree-lined thoroughfare that hugs the shoreline from the Dal Gate as far as the big hotels on the outskirts; and here the shikari 'boys', some in middle age, vie angrily with one another for the tourists' custom. The deal struck, the shikari boy then squats precariously at the furthermost tip of his boat and, paddle in hand, steers his passengers out into the lake. Many get back-handers from houseboat owners anxious for business, and requests to head for a particular vessel usually go unheard. The shikari boys are masters of persuasion, and passengers, intent only on finding somewhere to stay, often end up agreeing to a 2-hour trip around the lake, or to visiting one of the carpet factories in the labyrinth of waterways near the old part of the city.

At the Boulevard, Alison and Liz clambered into a shikari with their rucksacks and ended up at the houseboat *Sharin* in a back water reached by a channel thick, in places, with the dark green vegetation that would clog up the shallow lake, were it not removed. Compared with the floating palaces on the showier side of the lake, the *Sharin* was basic and scarcely more than a doonga, the shed-like boats on which the locals live and work. But it was clean and reasonably comfortable and the girls were delighted with their find.

'Houseboat is sublime,' Alison wrote in her diary.

The following morning the houseboy, Nagir, a man of about 40, brought the girls breakfast. It consisted, according to Liz's diary of 'good bits of most welcome chewy bread and Kashmiri honey'. Nagir said he would cook them anything they liked, even roast duck, but they explained their money wouldn't stretch to exotic dishes. Instead they got omelettes, cheese and yoghurt, and occasionally fish. They liked the food which was cooked in a hut at the rear of the houseboat and they had most of their meals on board.

Four years later I visited the *Sharin*. From my shikari I stepped onto the deck and was greeted by a man wearing a white, loosely fitting tunic of the type common in Kashmir. The pine planks of the deck had been bleached almost white by the sun and over the narrow entrance to the living quarters was a blue sign with 'H. B. Sharin' painted in yellow and white. I asked the man if he was Nagir. He nodded, but I couldn't be sure he had understood my question or, that if he had, I had been given the correct answer. At his side were two young children, a boy and a girl.

The room in which I was standing had a richly patterned carpet, a couch and two easy chairs. There was also dining room furniture as this was where guests took their meals. On one wall was a picture frame on which were pinned the photographs of previous guests. I looked for photographs of Alison and Liz but in vain. Beyond the living room was a simple bedroom with two single beds. A door led into a small bathroom with a tin shower. Like all the houseboats the *Sharin* was made almost entirely of pine and its varnished interior made it look not unlike a log cabin. It was easy to see why the girls felt at ease here.

I asked the man in the white tunic if he remembered two girls who stayed there four years earlier. "Oh yes," he said, "the girl Alison MacDonald went missing in Sonamarg and her father came here to stay. He slept in the same bed and at night I hear him cry. He is very sad."

I felt annoyed with myself for doubting that this was, in fact, Nagir.

Alison and Liz spent their first full day in Srinagar relaxing after the rigours of the long journey from Agra. Liz took a shikari over to the Boulevard to visit the bank and in the evening, after supper, they sat on the deck and watched the sun go down.

The following day, Sunday, they were more active. 'Went to arts emporium,' wrote Liz, 'and bought Grandma's bauble – Rs 98! Then sat in a beautiful, colourful garden and watched lunch party. Went to the cafe but could not get the Kashmiri dried fruit, milk shake, Russian tea or the town sandwich. Probably just as well! Went to church, just the two of us. Sat barefoot at the foot of the minister, reading alternate verses from the Psalms. Then returned to excellent beanfeast and bread.'

The next day the girls walked the five miles along the lakeside to the Shalimar Gardens. The gardens were among many created by the Mogul emperors during their Islamic crusade across northern India in the centuries before British rule. These ones were built in 1616 by Emperor Jehangir for his wife, Nur Jahan. They consist of four terraces, one above the other, and are irrigated by means of a central stone channel through which water flows in a series of pools and cascades. From the top terrace there is a magnificent view of the lake.

From Shalimar the girls could see the Hari Parbat Fort and the Hazratbal Mosque on the west side of the lake. The fort, built in the 18th century, is situated on top of a 350-feet hill and its brick red walls can be seen for miles around. The mosque, a mixture of Mogul and Kashmiri architecture, is said to enshrine a hair of the prophet Mohammed, but for non-Muslims its most outstanding feature is the view it commands of the lake. Nearby is the Kashmir University campus and all around are apple orchards and walnut trees.

Liz noted that the mosque was 'dazzling white and then ethereal, hazy blue'.

A young German stayed on the *Sharin*, sleeping, the girls presumed, in the living room. But there were language barriers and communication was confined mainly to nodding and smiling. They spent five more days in Srinagar. Sometimes they'd wander round the handicraft shops near the Bund, or haggle with the traders in the open-air market over the price of an apple, or a cool drink. They also climbed the 1,000-feet Sankara Acharya hill at the top of which, apart from the radio mast, is a temple, said to date back to 200 BC. Hindus still worship there.

On their map they saw a village called Sonamarg on the way to Ladakh, a barren wilderness high in the mountains, close to the border with Tibet. It seldom rains in Ladakh and very little grows there but India wants to hold onto its most northerly outpost and the army is never far away. Between World War 1 and 1974 Ladakh was virtually closed to foreigners but since then it has been popular with trekkers and hardy tourists keen to see its many Buddhist temples and its strange, moonlike landscape. Sonamarg, 83 kilometres from Srinagar, is the last village of any size before the Zoji La pass through the Himalayas into Ladakh. At 9,000 feet, it's some 3,000 feet higher than Srinagar and the girls decided to go there, perhaps to go trekking, perhaps to try to find a way into Nepal.

The day before they left for Sonamarg they met a man called Omar Bashir. He owned a handicraft shop and Alison bought a cushion cover from him. Later he invited them to accompany him to the Hotel Shahenshah where they enjoyed kebabs and listened to Kashmiri music. Neither girl thought there was anything sinister about the occasion; in fact Liz wrote in her diary that it had been 'very nice'.

Later, however, Omar Bashir was to be closely questioned by Kenny MacDonald and also the police. What, they wanted to know, was his interest in the two girls?

29

On 15 August Alison and Liz got up early to catch the bus to Sonamarg. While stepping down from the houseboat to the waiting shikari Alison accidently slipped and she and her rucksack ended up in the lake. Everyone, including the shikari boy, had a good laugh. A couple of hours later Alison, her clothes almost dry by then, took her seat on the bus for the three-hour journey north.

Two days later she disappeared.

## 3

The Balfour Hospital is a ten-minute walk from the centre of Kirkwall in Orkney and it was there that I found Dr. Liz Merry in late July 1985. She had graduated in medicine from Aberdeen University a year earlier and this was her first job. Junior hospital doctors work long hours and as we talked in the simple annex room in which she lived, she was constantly being summoned by her 'bleeper' to deal with an admission to the wards or a broken limb in casualty.

She told me about the first couple of weeks of her holiday with Alison, in particular their days on the houseboat in Srinagar. It was clear from what she said that the two girls got on well together.

Then we talked about their decision to go to Sonamarg.

"We decided to head towards Ladakh with vague feelings that if we could get through to Nepal that way it would be tremendous. We knew it was going to be quite a grim journey. We wanted to do it at speed so as not to waste too much of our holiday time and that's what led us up to Sonamarg."

"Tell me about the bus journey from Srinagar."

"There were wooden seats. I remember seeing lovely looking Kashmiri men in their homespun clothes. Alison commented that Sam (her brother) would have thought that these men were absolutely great in their hats, rather like a bigger version of a papal cap, and their shawls and white trousers. Some were carrying sacks, maybe rice, and we saw trussed-up chickens. People seemed to carry their lunch on the hoof. It was a spectacular journey."

"What happened when you got to Sonamarg?"

"We found somewhere to stay. I think we did it through the tourist officer, not a particularly great character. He was about 5′ 6″ and he loved bureaucracy; the sort of person who enjoyed making you fill in forms in triplicate. He wore a pair of elevated shoes that looked like spatulas. I was rather rude about them – I think he wore them to make him feel taller and greater. I'm not sure if he directed us to our hotel or whether we found it on our own. It was on the roadside and not difficult to find. Come to think of it we probably wandered there on our own."

This was the Glacier Guest House. I asked Liz to describe it.

"It had a sort of verandah with a wooden front and an open bit where you could sit out and have your meals. Behind us were the rooms. I think Alison was glad to be away from Srinagar. We were both very happy. We wondered about being able to trek in the hills and asked the tourist officer about this, but he was pretty unhelpful. Someone said something about a ponyman and I think it was the next day when the ponyman actually appeared. We then discussed where we could go and the Kolahoi Glacier looked a good possibility because it wasn't too far away. The chap said that would be fine and he quoted us a price. I was very enthusiastic. We must have talked about it later because Alison felt it was money she didn't want to spend. She had slightly less than I, probably £30-£40 less.

"We were very keen that when we got to Nepal we should go trekking and maybe see Everest, so we wanted to save a little money for that. Alison thought it would be a bad decision to spend it on this now and regret it later."

"How did you feel when Alison said she didn't want to go?"

"I didn't give it very much thought. I've thought since that had it been the other way around I might have been concerned, being the older of the two. Had she said she wanted to go vaulting off into the blue I might have said 'Hey, this isn't on' because it seemed to me the more risky option. It didn't occur to me she'd be in any danger by staying in Sonamarg."

"Had you made a pact to stay together?"

"No I don't think we ever thought we might split up. When we were discussing whether I should go off to the glacier, she said 'Och, you go on,' so I did."

"How long were you away?"

"About three and a half days."

"Just you and the ponyman?"

"Yes."

"Arguably if anyone was in danger it was you."

"That's right. But that wasn't something that occurred to either of us."

"Did you ever feel at risk?"

"Only from diarrhoea!"

The trek to the glacier began soon after breakfast. There were two ponies; one to carry the provisions they would need, the other to carry Liz. The ponyman, Eulag Mohammed, walked the whole way. The two girls said goodbye to one another and Alison took a photograph of her friend setting off astride the pony.

"It was an amazing first night," recalled Liz. "We went up and up and stayed in a sheepman's hut which, in spite of my sad memories, is an experience that sticks in my mind. It was a sort of wooden house. The animals literally stayed in the back and there were two earthenware ovens, one on either side of the door. I think there were two separate families living there. There were about twelve people sleeping in the house; they slept in a row down the middle and being a guest I had a privileged position next to the small boy and next to the gangway. They were very poor people. They eat chapatis and drink salt tea which should be approached with caution. It's tea and milk, butter if you're really pushing the boat out. The rock salt made it pink and I thought that to show my appreciation of their very meagre hospitality I couldn't spurn their salt tea. It was frightful.

"At night the sheepman rolled out his blanket for my benefit. There was a boulder against the entrance. I lay down that night and realised the salt tea had not been a good idea. I knew I was going to have to get out but I couldn't move the boulder. I heaved at it, but nothing happened. I must have climbed over that boulder about six times that night!

"There was another amusing incident the next day. We were about 14,000 feet up when, in the distance, we could see what looked like Bedouin tents and shepherds. The ponyman was quite keen to stop because he liked smoking a hookah. Then this chap appeared. He was draped in a shawl and had a funny bandage wrapped round his head. He was obviously quite prosperous because he had a watch on and he was carrying a transistor radio. I suppose they must have been status symbols. Then, over the radio, came news from Delhi in marvellous English, about the test match at Old Trafford."

"What did you think of the Kolahoi Glacier when you got there?"

"It was very impressive. Perhaps I blame it for what happened, I don't know. We spent our second night at the top. It was a bit more civilised. There was a building rather like a youth hostel, it even had bedsteads. There must have been another route to the glacier because we met Swedish tourists who had a chicken. I hadn't eaten for a while because of my fragile state so I crashed in on their barbecue.

"Having seen the glacier we came down and we came down fast. It was a very long day. The ponyman was keen to make good progress because if we got right down to the bottom we could stay at his mother's house. We got down and made our way to the village where his mother lived. It was a two-storey building made of wood. Then I met his elderly mother who made a great fuss of going off to buy eggs so I could have them boiled. She showed me up to a room. It had an electric light and a beautiful white duvet. After being away for two nights trekking it was tremendous. I had my boiled eggs and talked to the family because they seemed quite interested in me. Some guy was praying in the corner.

"I didn't want to offend them but I was so tired I said I was going to bed. I lay down and after a short while I felt this terrible itch. I thought it was psychological but when I turned on the light I saw I was covered in ticks, literally. I managed to pick them of one by one and then I changed my clothes. It was absolutely frightful. I can't describe it.

"I seriously considered walking around the room all night but I was too tired so I went out onto the balcony and slept there."

"What happened when you arrived back in Sonamarg?"

"We got back the following day. I was very keen to describe the excitement to Alison whose plans had been to go for walks in the hills and look at flowers.

"I got back to the hotel. There were two Italians in the room next door. I asked them where my friend was and they said she had gone for a walk. I was a bit disappointed so I got the key and went into her room and decided I might as well do something practical. We'd have plenty of time over supper to exchange news.

"My washing was grim so I went down to the river to wash it – that's where people wash their clothes in Sonamarg. I bought a bar of soap and had quite an active afternoon. At about half past five, maybe five, I thought it a bit strange that Alison hadn't returned from her walk so I had a word with the Italian couple again and a young lad who seemed to be looking after the hotel.

"It was only then it became clear she had gone for her walk on the Monday, the day after I left. She'd been missing for three nights."

# 4

As he sat in the departure lounge at Heathrow Airport waiting for Air India flight 116 to Delhi a thousand thoughts flashed through Kenny MacDonald's mind. Was Alison simply lost? Might she have decided to stay put in a remote village until help arrived? Or was she already dead, the victim of a sex fiend, or a wild animal or the awesome mountains of Kashmir? In his diary he wrote:

> Oh Alison, please hold on till I come. Lord, Lord have mercy upon us. Help us to accept Thy will, but please, please be merciful to Alison.

Soon the Boeing 747 was airborne and cruising at 35,000 feet. The nine-hour flight over Copenhagen and Moscow was the most direct route and there were no stopovers. Kenny realised he had been lucky to get a seat at such short notice. Lunch, or was it dinner – meals never seem to come in the right order on these long-haul flights – was good. The main course was turkey and afterwards, when they showed a movie starring Glenda Jackson, he even relaxed a little.

He drifted between sleep and consciousness, his mind in turmoil. He awoke suddenly and startled Ian Merry, a 54-year-old computer engineer, who was sitting next to him. Less than 48 hours before, the two men had been going about their very different lives at opposite ends of the country; now they had been thrown together by circumstances neither could have foreseen.

Kenny thought back to the phone call he'd received from Ian Merry. He and Reta were watching television at their home in the Marchmont area of Edinburgh. It was about 10 o'clock on Saturday night.

"Hello, this is Ian Merry, Elisabeth's father. I'm afraid I've got some very bad news."

He then read out the international cable message he'd received a short time before. It read. 'Alison missing six days in hill in spite search. Contact Mr MacDonald, 39 Thirlestane

Rd., Edinburgh. Advise. Reply: Post Office Sonamarg, Kashmir.'

Kenny was numbed, but he had to think and act quickly. He told Reta straight away and she had to draw on all her strength to stay calm. Derek, at 12, was too young to take in the fact that his sister was missing, possibly dead. Sam, five years Derek's elder, was given the news when he returned home a short time later. They all prayed. Kenny found the verse in Psalm 50 he had been looking for. It began: 'Call upon me in the day of trouble.' At their home in the Hampshire village of Hartley Wintney, Ian Merry and his wife Rosemary wondered what, if anything, they could do to help. They rang a neighbour who had climbed in the Himalayas and another neighbour, who knew the area well, produced photographs of Kashmir, including Sonamarg.

Ian called Kenny again to tell him he had been in touch with the Foreign Office but that there was no news. Kenny had also called but it was late and he was told to try again at 9.30 the following morning. He'd already decided to fly to India at the first opportunity.

That night Ian and Rosemary stayed up till 2 a.m. discussing whether he, too, should go. What if Alison was dead? Their own daughter, although not in any kind of danger herself, would need support and protection. They couldn't expect a bereaved father to provide that. There was only one thing to do: Ian must go too.

That night the MacDonalds slept very little. For Kenny, morning couldn't come quickly enough. At five he got up, washed, had a cup of tea and started planning his trip to India.

At this point he didn't know Liz's father had decided to join him. That night he wrote in his diary: 'I am too scared to go to India', but his fear was based on what he might find when he got there, rather than the thought of travelling on his own.

Two of his five sisters, Peggy and Morag, and one of his brothers, Roddy, lived not very far away in Edinburgh and they all came round on being given the news. Another brother, Donald, came over from Glasgow and provided some useful information. He happened to be the assistant secretary of the Highland Fund, an organisation set up to provide low-interest loans to crofters and fishermen. The secretary of the fund was a man called Roderick MacFarquhar whose brother, Sir

Alexander MacFarquhar, had had a distinguished career in the Indian Civil Service and was a personal friend of the Governor of Kashmir, B. K. Nehru. A telephone call to Sir Alexander that morning produced the result Donald had hoped for and later, when Kenny was in Kashmir investigating his daughter's disappearance, he found the introduction to the Governor to be extremely useful when it came to cutting through Indian red tape.

One of the first people to be contacted that morning was the Reverend Alastair Ross, minister of Buccleuch and Greyfriars Free Church in Edinburgh and a friend of the MacDonalds. He announced during the morning service that Alison was missing and by evening a fund had already started. One anonymous member of the congregation, an elder, even offered to 'pick up the tab' for Kenny's visit to India.

The MacDonalds, themselves, were virtually penniless. Financial hardship was one of the crosses they had to bear as a result of Kenny's decison to train for the ministry. But Peggy's husband, Fred, gave £200 and there were cheques and cash from other relatives and friends.

His diary entry for that day, 23 August, said:

Oh Alison, where are you?... I can't really get through to God. He has cut himself off from me and yet He must be guiding me. Was it my fault? . . . Phoned Alastair Ross for prayers in church. Could hardly say anything. Very sympathetic.

Only one member of the family hadn't been told the news. Mairi, Alison's elder sister, lived in Stornoway with her husband, Donald, and was expecting her second child. It was decided that Reta should have the heart-breaking task of telling her.

Phone Mairi? No – Reta. Poor Reta does not want to tell Mairi any sooner than necessary.

Morag made lunch but Kenny's mouth was dry and his stomach was in a knot. He ate but didn't enjoy the meal. That afternoon Donald drove his brother to Edinburgh Airport for the flight south.

When Kenny arrived at Heathrow that evening Ian and Rosemary Merry were there to meet him. The flight to Delhi was the following morning, so they all went back to the Merry's home in Hampshire. Mrs Merry prepared a light supper of roast beef sandwiches and fruit while the two men talked about the trip that lay ahead of them. Earlier she'd picked some sweet peas from the garden and put them in a vase in Kenny's room. That night, as he tried to sleep, he thought about his family back in Edinburgh:

> Bed – thinking of Sam, Derek and Reta. Sam so tall and strong as he shook my hand – a good lad with a heart of gold. Reta concerned for me. She's strong and capable despite her heartbreak. Derek? Who knows what he's thinking but he was a great pal of Alison's. God bless them all. How about Mairi? Poor dear Mairi. So close to Alison in age yet different. How they used to laugh. Lord, please soften this blow to us . . . What if Sam is right and Alison is already in a better place?

In the morning he rose at 6.30, had tea in his room, and within an hour he and Ian were on their way to Heathrow for the flight to Delhi.

The search for Alison had begun.


"Mr MacDonald?"

"Yes."

"My name is Stephen Hampson from the British High Commission. Would you follow me, please." It was 9 p.m. local time, but the gust of hot air that hit the passengers the moment the aircraft doors opened indicated that the temperature was still in the high 70s, maybe more.

At night, Delhi International Airport looks decidedly down-at-heel, a far cry from the plush plazas of, say, Frankfurt or New York's JFK and the unwelcome feeling is compounded by the long, exasperating wait to get through Immigration Control. But, on this occasion, the khaki-uniformed officers must have been in a benevolent mood for Kenny and his companion were able to complete the formalities relatively quickly.

Outside, the three men pushed through the converging scrum of taxi drivers and made their way to Stephen Hampson's official car. Already Kenny was sweating and he realised Delhi in August is not a place to wear a tweed jacket. He saw men sprawled over car bonnets; they appeared to be asleep. And as he dodged the advancing army of street vendors he wondered whether Alison had come this way four weeks earlier.

Stephen Hampson, a civil servant in the British High Commission's economics section, had been briefed on the case, and as they were being driven the eight miles into the city, he told the two men what he knew of Kashmir and its people. At the High Commission, Gurkhas saluted as they drove in through the open gates and headed towards the building in which the young diplomat, his Swedish wife, Gunilla, and their three children had a flat. The children had been moved into the couple's own bedroom for the night so Kenny and Ian could each have their own room. By this time it was 1.30 a.m., and Kenny decided to phone Reta. How good, he thought, to hear her voice. Gunilla gave them something to eat as they discussed the day ahead. The two hosts said there was absolutely no history of women being molested in Kashmir, certainly not European women. But the deep anxiety that weighed heavily on Kenny's mind, remained.

In the morning the visitors were awoken by the children. Kenny forgot a cardinal rule of India – never clean your teeth with tap water. But he didn't drink any and reckoned he would be safe. Breakfast consisted of a boiled egg, rolls and coffee. The egg was small and the yoke, a pale, anaemic yellow.

That morning the two men were introduced to Miss Mary McLaren, a consular official. She was sympathetic but unable to add anything to their knowledge of the situation. They were given the name of John Ray, headmaster of the Tyndale Biscoe Mission School in Srinagar. He was a kind of unofficial British representative in Kashmir and it was felt that he might be able to help.

It was very hot. There were a few hours to kill before the flight north and Ian bought a small guidebook of Kashmir and Ladakh. They saw some of New Delhi's impressive official buildings and Stephen Hampson pointed out trees planted by famous people, the most recent by Prince Charles. Then they returned to the Hampson's flat and, after coffee, Gunilla drove them to the airport.

"What's the rule of the road, here?" inquired Ian.

"Biggest goes first," was the reply. "No one gives way to anything smaller, no matter how vulnerable."

At Delhi's domestic air terminal there was a long queue for

the 13½-hour flight to Srinagar. Ian got the tickets and was relieved to discover he could pay for them with his American Express card. Two days earlier, on the Sunday, he'd been able to raise £150 on his and Rosemary's cash cards, but that was all the cash he had with him.

Waiting to go through the security check, Kenny spoke to some Indians and a South African woman. He noticed that some of the police and customs officials had pot bellies which seemed to be accentuated by the big leather belts around their middles. Kashmir is popular with Indian as well as foreign tourists and the Indian Airlines flight was full. Attractive hostesses in sarees came round with a tray of sweets and later they served a cold snack, rather like a curried Scotch egg minus the egg. Kenny enjoyed it. He picked up a copy of *The Times of India* and a story caught his attention: 'A Pakistan ladies' hockey team yesterday withdrew from the Asia Tournament as it is unlawful for Muslim women to perform in front of spectators in shorts where there are men.' He pondered whether it was the women or the spectators who were wearing the shorts, but he got the gist and, smiling to himself, wondered what old MacDougall, a particularly strict Free Church elder in Lewis, would have made of it all.

Through the windows the two men could see the ragged, snow-capped peaks of the Himalaya range. Below were the green fields and forests of Kashmir. Kenny felt relieved. He had expected to see a wilderness. If Alison was still alive, he thought, she would have a better chance of surviving here. The aircraft landed on the plateau on which Srinagar's airport is built and as the two men walked across to the crowded, single-storey terminal they appreciated the cooler temperature of Kashmir after the heavy, stifling heat of Delhi. They took a taxi into town and as it thundered along at high speed Ian realised what Gunilla Hampson had meant about the law of the road, as rickshaw drivers and pedestrians scrambled out of the way in the nick of time. The taxi took them to the tourist centre, there being nowhere open at the airport where they could convert sterling into rupees.

From the tourist centre it was only a short walk to the Tyndale-Biscoe Mission School. John Ray, headmaster since 1962, lived with his wife Catherine, in a detached house in the grounds. The two men asked for directions and a gaggle of small, excitable boys, vied with one another for the honour of accompanying the visitors to the headmaster's crumbling edifice among the trees.

The day begins at Tyndale-Biscoe with Christian prayers, a curious ritual as most of the 1,300 boys are Muslims. But this is India, where the British, and particularly their institutions, are still revered and in Srinagar there is considerable prestige and kudos to be gained from sending your son to the school, even though the copy of the New Testament he will receive, on leaving, will probably never be opened, let alone understood.

John Ray does not see his role as that of converter. Instead, he prefers the approach adopted in 1890 by the school's founder who said he wanted to see the boys morally 'lifted up' by attending his classes. Hence, the school places great emphasis on mountaineering and rowing, and other pursuits deemed to be character building. And were it not for the dusky skins of the boys and the black kites hovering above the sun-baked grass, the Tyndale Biscoe could easily pass for an English public school; or even for Gordonstoun, at which John Ray once taught.

Beyond the open-air swimming pool, in which boys in underpants learn how to stay afloat in preparation for another of the school's rituals, the weekly rowing regatta on the Dal Lake, is the headmaster's house. The two men introduced themselves to John Ray and were invited in. He had been told to expect them and had already written to the police at Sonamarg. Kenny told him what little he knew about Alison's disappearance, adding that he had an introduction to the Governor of Kashmir, B. K. Nehru. The headmaster immediately phoned the Governor's secretary, only to be told that Mr Nehru was at lunch and couldn't be disturbed. Kenny, determined that the authorities shouldn't delay a thorough search any longer, demanded that the Governor be told right away, even at lunch, and mentioned the name of Sir Alexander MacFarquhar. A few minutes later the secretary rang back to say the Governor would see him there and then.

Under clause 370 of the Indian constitution, the state of Jammu & Kashmir is given special status and enjoys a relatively high degree of autonomy. It has its own legislature and Acts passed in Delhi have to be approved by the government of Jammu & Kashmir before becoming law. The Governor is appointed by the Indian Parliament and has a role not unlike that of a monarch; he is the supreme legal authority but, in practice, the law of the land is decided by the lower and upper Houses of the State Legislature – the Assembly and the Council. As with many of India's institutions, the legal system is based on the British model.

The Governor's Residence is a large, Edwardian country house of considerable charm and elegance. It overlooks the Dal Lake some eight miles north of Srinagar and is surrounded by stout, gnarled walnut trees where, in early October, peasants, many of them children, gather the still-green nuts blown down by the first of the autumn winds.

The two men arrived by taxi and a uniformed military aide saluted, and invited them to take a seat on the verandah.

Within a matter of minutes they were ushered into the room where the Governor was waiting for them. The Governor had heard about Alison's disappearance and promised to give whatever practical help he could. He instructed his secretary to call the Director-General of police, a man called Watali, and asked an aide to provide him with daily reports. The visitors felt he was attentive, to the point and genuinely concerned. The meeting lasted an hour, after which they returned to the mission school where John Ray introduced them to his wife, Catherine, whom he met in Pakistan while they were both doing missionary work, he as a teacher, she as a doctor working for the Church of Scotland.

The four discussed what might have happened to Alison. Could she have been molested, or even killed, by pilgrims returning a week earlier from the annual 'Yatra' to the Amarnath Cave at the head of the Sindh Valley and only a two-day trek from Sonamarg? The occasion is a major event in the Hindu calendar and thousands make the punishing and sometimes dangerous climb to the cave, 13,000 feet up a mountain thirty miles from the town of Pahalgam. At night the temperature falls to below zero, and exposure and exhaustion take their toll on the elderly and infirm. Near the top, the mud turns to snow and ice, but ascetics, barefooted and almost naked, appear oblivious to the conditions. Ponies and mules, weighted down with supplies and cooking utensils, trudge disconsolately upwards under their owners' sticks, and the wealthy and decadent puff and sweat under their own excessive weight. The very rich employ coolies to do their sweating for them. At the cave the pilgrims pass one by one in front of a natural ice lingham, or phallus, the symbol of the Lord Shiva, one of Hinduism's holiest gods.

In August 1981 was it possible that pilgrims returning from the Yatra saw a pretty European girl, alone, in Sonamarg and pounced? Kenny thought it was out of the question and John Ray considered it unlikely. But in Ian Merry's mind a doubt lingered.

A police car arrived at the mission school to take the two men to Sonamarg. John Ray suggested a Kashmiri teacher at the school, a man called Vakil, should go with them. Vakil was, like John Ray, an experienced climber, and it was felt his knowledge of the area could be useful. The rest of the party comprised the driver and a police superintendent. Ian thought he was probably in his early fifties but looked older.

As they left the Rays' home, the superintendent asked the others if they would mind first stopping off at his home so he could change his shoes. The drive took them through some of Srinagar's poorer suburbs to where the policeman lived with his family and elderly parents. The old man, reclining on a sofa, received the visitors and a polite conversation ensued, the son acting as interpreter. Small cakes and glasses of sweet, milky tea were produced and Kenny found himself having to give a time-consuming explanation why he was in Kashmir. The two men, while appreciative of the hospitality, were anxious to be on their way and could have done without this delay. But it was an interesting insight into Kasmiri family life and Ian felt the occasion exhibited considerable patriarchal dignity.

At last they were off, this time in a different direction. The superintendent was obsessed with the need to keep in constant contact by radio and every few minutes, it seemed, the call sign 'Hotel 07' crackled over the airwaves. The superintendent spoke as though he'd picked up the jargon from watching too many episodes of *Z Cars*, embellishing some of the phrases for extra affect. Hence, his messages invariably ended: "Roger, over and out and over." Kenny and Ian were relieved when the radio eventually packed in.

The bumpy road took them along the bottom of the Sindh Valley, in which lies some of Kashmir's most spectacular scenery. The Sindh River flows down from the Amarnath and Haramukh glaciers into the Anchar Lake and on either side the mountains rise steeply, their purple and brown peaks occasionally revealing small patches of white. Chinar trees line the road, sometimes giving way to poplar, walnut, apple and almond and in spring cherry adds to the striking softness of the different shades of blossom.

Kenny was deep in thought. He had no idea what to expect in Sonamarg. His daughter might be dead, her body already found. In little more than an hour he might be faced with the agonising task of identifying the remains of his beloved Alison. After that, there would be the long, sad journey back to Scotland with her body and her belongings. He didn't know if he could face it. He prayed, silently, that she would be found alive and unharmed.

Darkness was falling fast as they drove through Kangan, stopping, briefly, at a police check point for a glass of tea and another chat. At one point the driver failed to see a diversion sign, bringing the car to a sudden halt only feet from disaster. The bridge that had previously stood there had been washed away in a flood and now there was nothing. When Ian saw the place in daylight a few days later he wondered how they hadn't all been killed.

They finally arrived in Sonamarg at 9.30 p.m. and went straight to the police station, a wooden hut at the far end of the village. The officer in charge was an assistant inspector called Maharaj Krishun Machama. He was tall and Ian thought his moustache made him look a little like David Niven.

It was worse than Kenny had thought. Alison had left the Glacier Guest House at 10 a.m. eight days earlier, apparently to go for a short walk. She was wearing only blue jeans, a blue checked shirt and brown, lacing shoes. Round her waist she had tied her mother's blue kagool and she was wearing her mother's Zandor wrist watch. Her only other possession was a small, navy suede purse attached to a shoulder strap. No one knows what was in the purse, but her pen and writing pad were not among her belongings when her room at the guest house was searched several days later; nor was a letter to Ian

44

and Rosemary Merry which their daughter had asked Alison to post for her. The post box was only 100 yards away, but the letter never arrived. The only other fact the police had been able to establish was that she crossed the street to a fruit stall and bought three apples.

A policeman had been sent off to fetch Liz Merry who had remained in the village to await the arrival of Kenny. She didn't know her father would also be there. Meanwhile Inspector Machama, a Hindu, continued his account of the police investigation up to that point. He struck the two men as being competent and with a good grasp of the situation. Liz arrived, and seeing a man in the corner of the dimly lit hut, assumed him to be Alison's father. It was only when he stood up that she realised it was her own father. She sobbed, briefly, and they hugged one another. She then told her story; how she and Alison had discussed going to the glacier together and how her friend decided, in the end, against it. And she described what happened when she got back from her three-day trek to find Alison no longer there.

## 5

Four years later, in Orkney, Liz recalled what she told them that night.

"I went to the police station and waited. Eventually the inspector arrived. He was the one my father called David Niven. I remember thinking thank heavens he speaks good English. I sat down on the floor, cross-legged – eventually he brought a chair – and I started to fill in these forms in triplicate. About five-sixths of the way through my story someone came in to say a European girl had been seen. I felt absolutely great. But then I realised something was wrong; the description was wrong, the place was wrong. I just burst into tears.

"Maharaj, the inspector, came forward and put his arm round me and I felt that this chap actually cared. He had children of his own and later on I always felt he was someone who was with me. Kenny doesn't support Maharaj as wholeheartedly as I do but, of course, he was not there, then, on his own."

"Did Maharaj give any indication what he thought had happened to Alison?"

"No. At first we got the practical things underway. We ascertained fairly quickly that the first thing she had done was buy three apples. Then he got his constables, of whom he hadn't very many – about six – and sent them up onto the hills; there were lights on the hills that night. Some of the constables were better than others, but generally they did a useful job."

"Then what happened?"

"Two girls arrived, I think they were British, and asked if they could do anything. They were going down to Srinagar so I asked them if they could send a telegram to my father. The telegram went off saying 'Alison missing six days in hills in spite search. Contact Mr MacDonald, 39 Thirlestane Road, Edinburgh. Advise. Reply Post Office, Sonamarg, Kashmir'."

"What did you think had happened to Alison at that point?"

"I just didn't know. My main concern was that if she was up in the hills she would be jolly cold. I was very worried. Other possibilities have gone through my mind since, but at the time that was my main thought."

"Where did you begin the search?"

"One of the first places we looked was the river. I went out
with a constable and we walked quite a long way up the river,
but the going got too tough and we had to turn back. Another
day we went up the road towards Leh with the inspector and
came back on a tractor. It was raining and I remember singing
'She'll be coming round the mountain'. Maharaj didn't know
what to make of it all and asked me if I was praying!"

"How thorough was the police effort?"

"Well at that time they didn't have a lot of scope. There
were only six constables, but I think Maharaj did as well as
he could. It was very unusual for anyone to go missing and I
think he was horrified; I certainly got that feeling. We both
felt that she had intended to only go for a short walk. You
don't set out to go over to Pakistan if you've only got a pair
of light shoes and three apples. She definitely didn't plan on
going for a long walk. When we arrived in the village Alison
pointed out the river to me, so that was where we started
looking for her."

"Did the police think she may have been abducted?"

"No, they said that didn't happen in Kashmir. It may have
been more common in other parts of India but not there. Of
course, perhaps they just wanted to defend their own territory.
There was nothing at all to suggest she had been abducted. The
fellow in the hotel seemed very pleasant, although the hotel
owner was a slightly shadowy figure in the background."

"What happened next?"

"I got a telegram saying 'Kenneth MacDonald coming out
with assistance'. I had vague visions of this man I'd never met
plus the Household Cavalry. The night he arrived I was woken
in my hotel room at 11.30 and I was walked down the dark
street by the police constable. I had never met Alison's parents,
although I had seen them briefly on a station platform. At the
police station I had expected to see only Kenneth and I had
this awful thought of meeting someone whose daughter you
were responsible for having disappeared. As I walked into the
police officer's room I saw a man sitting on a chair. The lighting
was poor and I assumed it was Mr MacDonald, but when he
got up I saw it was my Dad. I remember shedding tears of
relief. At that point there was a quiet approach from behind

47

and a hand laid on my shoulder. It was Kenny. He said, 'How are you? Are you all right?' He was genuinely concerned for me. It was unbelievable."

"You mentioned that you felt awful about meeting Alison's father. Did you feel responsible for her disappearance?"

"I felt badly about it. Had I been there, instead of going off to the glacier, it probably wouldn't have happened. Yes, I feel an element of responsibility. Looking back, I think it was unwise of us to separate."

"Do you think Alison is still alive?"

"I doubt it. I have never shared Ken's conviction, and he knows that. I would certainly never say that she was dead and if she were found it would be great. But I suppose ever since I left India I regarded that as unlikely. I've tried not to be dishonest in this respect and I think he knows my feelings. If she is alive and reappears, it would be so wonderful. I think we would all be a bit different."

There was limited accommodation in the village and after Liz had given her version of events, she, her father and Kenny MacDonald all went back to her room in the Glacier Guest House. Kenny was anxious to find out as much as possible that night and got the manager and the room boy to tell him what they knew. As they talked late into the night it became clear that the last people to have seen Alison before she set off on her walk were an Italian couple staying in the room next door. Kenny established that the Italians left Sonamarg soon after Alison disappeared, but where were they now? He decided they would have to be traced and interviewed.

The guest house was nothing more than a wooden hut – Ian likened it to a small, broken-down cricket pavilion – and the facilities were basic to say the least. There were three single beds in the wooden-floored room. Kenny knelt by his bed to pray and climbed into his daughter's sleeping bag to try to get some sleep in preparation for the hard day's walking ahead of him. Ian found the high altitude was not conducive to sleep and lay awake thinking about what Liz had said earlier. She had, he thought, given a clear account of events as she saw them; of leaving on the pony trek nine days previously; of arranging to meet Alison at the hotel the following Thursday at around

*Alison MacDonald*

*Alison MacDonald, aged 11 in Lewis,*
*with brothers Derek (centre) and Sam*

*Alison MacDonald, student in Aberdeen*

*Kenny MacDonald leading search party
at Sonamarg, Kashmir, September 1981.*

*Fruit stall, Sonamarg, at which Alison bought
3 apples on morning she disappeared*

*Kenny MacDonald at Gurais, Kashmir, November 1983.*

*Police Superintendent, Javed Machdoomi*

4 p.m.; of her return that day at midday; of the Italian couple who said Alison had gone for a walk; of her concern in the evening when there was still no sign of her; and of finding out from the Italians that she had gone for her walk, not that day, but three days earlier on the Monday. Ian Merry reflected, also, on how Liz had reacted: she had shown initiative, courage and maturity. He was proud of his daughter.

Kenny had also been impressed with her handling of the situation. His diary entry for Tuesday 25 August included the following:

> Elisabeth Merry brought. Delightful surprise to find her father there
> – cries in arms. I shake hands; small girl, pretty face, well-spoken:
> ignores own hardship and immediately sympathises with me.

As he lay in bed, his mind racing, he went over and over again the story that was beginning to unfold. He considered why Alison didn't go with Liz to the glacier. Was it because she could not afford to go?

> Why did I not give her more money; but I did not have any more to give.

Or was it because it would have meant leaving on a Sunday, the Sabbath?

> That's why Alison would not go. She really was a good Christian.

He thought back on what Liz had told him earlier; how she immediately went to the police and how, the next day, there was a full search of the locality. In his diary he wrote:

> Up to hotel room; Alison's comb, clothes, maps, camera, Bible – all
> Alison's but no Alison. Search of room; examine travellers cheques –
> relieved, plenty of money. Sabbath observance kept her back. Question
> hotel people. Barlow (police superintendent) a nut; Niven appears to
> have done all. Tea etc. Off to bed in Alison's sleeping bag. Where are
> you Alison? Oh Lord, Lord, give us peace of mind to look tomorrow.
> Maybe she's sick in a village somewhere. The bed is hard, but
> comfortable; lantern light; toilet, an open hole in the floor. Did you
> enjoy being here Alison? Where are you now? Wild animal? Bears in
> the woods? Would you run away? Would you have a chance? If she
> was killed by a bear please, Lord, let it have been quick. Please don't
> let her suffer. What if she was kidnapped?

That night he was in a state of anguish as he contemplated the prospect of never seeing his daughter again. But in one sense he was at peace; for the first time since being told of Alison's disappearance, he had finally managed to get through to God.

# 6

My second visit to the MacDonalds' home at Rosskeen was
in early September 1985. The couple's eldest son, Sam, had
returned from Kashmir only a couple of days earlier, and was
travelling up from London that day. His train was due to arrive
at Inverness at about midday and Kenny had arranged to drive
the 22 miles there, in his ageing white Volvo estate to collect
him. We had about an hour and a half to talk so I used the
time to ask him about what was going through his mind when
he arrived in Sonamarg. Did he begin the search right away,
I enquired?

"Yes. We didn't arrive up there till very late but it was
important that I started the questioning that night to get a
general picture of things. I saw Alison's own room and found
out various things so that at first light in the morning, about
six, I was ready to go outside and see what the terrain was like."

"What were Ian Merry's thoughts when you reached
the village?"

"I think he was pessimistic. He, I suppose, was overwhelmed
with relief that his own daughter was fine and that he was
going to see her. I suppose he wouldn't have had too much
time to think about Alison. But on the whole I think he was
too matter-of-fact to accept that there was any hope. Anyone
going on facts and going on all that we knew would come to
the same conclusion – that there was no hope."

"What were Liz's feelings when you first met her?"

"Liz was really tremendous. I can't speak too highly about
her because she had gone through an awful experience, losing
her friend who was with her there and coming back to all the
turmoil; being interrogated by the police for hours on end and
going out and physically looking for Alison and expecting to
find her maybe dead at any moment, and then trying to contact
her parents and wondering what our reaction would be."

"But how did she feel about it all?"

"They had a degree of responsibility to each other but I suppose
that if anyone had extra responsibility it would have been Liz
because she was the elder of the two and had travelled widely

before. But it was really something the way she stood up to all of this. Her thoughts on the matter? Well, she just couldn't understand it. There was no reason whatsoever why Alison should disappear and nor could she see any reason why Alison might have been taken away. It was just absolutely perplexing to her."

"Did you sense, in Liz, a feeling of guilt?"

"No. No guilt whatsoever but I think she was quite perturbed as to what reaction I might have. And I think she was very relieved to see that my reaction was sympathy for her predicament. I could see what she had gone through and I think she was vastly relieved that I treated it in that way."

"How much did she regret going off to the glacier?"

"When something happens each one of us says 'if only'; it's a kind of personal torture. But you can't change life and you can't do things in retrospect. I'm sure Liz feels very guilty about a whole range of things but then don't we all feel guilty? Maybe Reta and I shouldn't have let Alison go in the first place. But you can't go through life like that. You make a decision and you face up to the consequences."

"In Sonamarg, how did you begin your search?"

"I used the first few days to reconnoitre the area because I just wanted to see the lie of the land and work out where I thought Alison would have gone for a walk. But at the back of my mind I was also looking for places where she might have been attacked and her body buried so I was also keeping my eye open for freshly dug areas of ground and dangerous places where her body could have been deposited."

"Of all the possibilities that went through your mind which did you think was the most probable?"

"When I saw the area I thought it was a crime of passion in which she had been attacked and her body disposed of somewhere round about."

"By whom?"

"I didn't know the area or the people well enough so I had an open mind, but probably by the troops that passed through here. A lot of troops are stationed in the area and they do stop off at Sonamarg."

"So you thought she had been raped and killed by soldiers?"

"That's right. Yes."

"Did anything else point to this conclusion?"

"No; I just thought that with a nice-looking girl, out on her own, the possibility was high that she might have been attacked, raped and left for dead."

"By the military?"

"Well I had no reason to believe that but, thinking of our own army, there are always a couple of bad eggs who would do that sort of thing."

It was almost time for Kenny to leave for Inverness to pick up Sam. Reta had decided to go with him, leaving me alone in the house. He said they'd be away for about an hour and left me to pick my way through literally hundreds of documents, newspaper cuttings, maps and correspondence concerning Alison's disappearance. They were kept, in no particular order, in a big plastic sack.

I sensed that no one outside the family had ever seen these papers. It was only when I started reading them that I realised why. The material in that innocuous looking sack revealed far more about the case than had ever been made public: the secret meetings with informants; the danger to which Kenny had been exposed; the forays into politically sensitive areas; the extraordinary 'dream' of a family friend; the list of suspects and, most of all, the sleuth-like cunning of this clergyman turned detective.

I became so absorbed in the documents that I didn't hear the car pull up outside. The London train was on time and Sam, an art student in London, had spent the 25-minute journey to Rosskeen telling his parents about his three-week holiday in Kashmir with his girlfriend, Fiona.

They'd stayed on a houseboat in Srinagar, gone to Sonamarg for a day and spent some time with the Rays at the mission school. But there were simply no new leads at all about Alison's disappearance.

There was one piece of happy news, though. To his parents' delight Sam announced that he and Fiona had got engaged on their return.

Sonamarg can scarcely be described as a pretty village. It means 'meadow of gold', a reference to the carpet of small alpine flowers that adorn the lower slopes in summer. But the village itself is little more than a collection of tawdry shops and dubious tea stalls. On the hillside a few timber bungalows, painted green, offer basic accommodation and, near the new tourist centre, scrawny trekking ponies seek out any remaining blades of grass. Once it was an important trading post on the route linking India and central Asia. But nowadays its main role, apart from tourism, is as a stopping-off point for the convoys of military vehicles travelling to and from the cease-fire line which separates the – occasionally – warring armies of India and Pakistan.

From late October until April or May Sonamarg is virtually cut off from the outside world. Depending on the severity of the winter, some local hillpeople, the Gujars, might remain, sharing their wooden and stone shelters with their cattle. But when the tourists go, so too do the traders who journey south in search of work, or return to their businesses in Srinagar and Jammu.

The village has the appearance and feel of being just on the edge of civilisation which, in a sense, it is. The road that now carries daily convoys of Indian troops was built in 1962 after a major border conflict with China, and visitors travelling beyond Sonamarg through the Zoji La pass could be forgiven for wondering whether they had strayed onto another planet by mistake.

Sonamarg is really two villages. The first consists of just one street running parallel to the Sindh river. On one side, traders compete for business from a row of stalls and shops selling many of the things Kashmir is famous for – shawls, wood carvings, silks, papier mache, furs and jewellery. Restaurants and tea stalls make up the remainder of the timber and corrugated iron buildings. Opposite is the village 'Arts Emporium' and on the same side of the street stands the Glacier Guest House. The indigenous population of Sonamarg live in a cluster of mainly wooden homes on the opposite side of the river, a ten-minute walk from where the tourist buses stop. The modern bridge, built by the army, is made of concrete and is sturdy enough to take the heavy military vehicles that cross it daily. Sonamarg is at an altitude of 9,000 feet and the lush pastures of the Kashmir valley have already given way to the harsh terrain of the Himalayas. Beyond are the barren wastes of Ladakh where 18,000-feet mountains present a formidable barrier to passing rain clouds and very little grows there. The people, whose culture, appearance and religion owes more to Tibet than India, have to eke out whatever living their simple economy allows.

I arrived in Sonamarg in late September 1985 and already the shopkeepers were preparing to leave. In a month it would be almost deserted. Beyond the Glacier Guest House, on the same side of the road, is the police station and in front of the now flaking green paintwork of the tourist centre twenty or thirty tethered ponies waited, wearily, as their owners sought tourists keen to add trekking to their list of holiday experiences.

Sonamarg is probably the best known trekking centre in Kashmir. From here, many hundreds of young adventurers set out every summer for climbs of varying degrees of difficulty. The six-day trek to Wangat, for example, reaches, at one point, an altitude of 13,000 feet, and the thin mountain air soon fatigues the unclimatised lowlander. At the opposite end of the scale there is a comfortable two-mile walk to Thajiwas, a valley at the foot of the Sonamarg glacier. But even here danger lurks for anyone tempted onto the steep slopes leading to the solid mass of grey snow that the locals ambitiously call a glacier.

It was here, among the meadows and mountains of northern Kashmir, that Kenny MacDonald began his search for his daughter on Wednesday 26 August 1981.

That morning he rose early, about 6 a.m., and went outside to look around. It was the first time he had seen the area in daylight. The sheer, terrifying beauty of the place filled him with foreboding. If she were out there, alone, how could she possibly have survived?

Sitting at a table on the dilapidated verandah, Ian, Liz and Kenny breakfasted on curds, omelettes, tea and Kashmiri bread. The hotel owner and his two assistants seemed friendly enough, but were clearly worried. That morning the three Britons drove about three miles along the road towards Ladakh. With them were the police superintendent whom Kenny had nicknamed 'Barlow' and the moustachioed inspector that reminded Ian of David Niven. They passed the military camp, on the other side of the bridge, but didn't go in. And they stopped to make a cursory search of a shallow lake, noting to make a thorough search later. Nearby, the river was in spate. On one side was a steep bank. That night Kenny wrote in his diary:

55

Oh, Alison, did you fall in and were you swept away? You'd be stopped by these boulders, surely, my darling. I hope whatever happened it was quick.

They stopped a lorry carrying soldiers and asked whether they had seen a European girl along the road. They said they had seen a girl on her own at Kargil 80 miles away in Ladakh. Kenny, excited by this information, showed them a photograph of Alison. No, came the reply, that wasn't the girl.

The altitude had affected Ian and in the afternoon, as he rested, the others set off along the river bank. The going got increasingly tough but Kenny's fitness enabled him to cover a lot of ground quickly. The sweat was pouring off him and as they climbed higher he felt sick as he looked down at the angry river below. Some time before a woman and child had fallen to their deaths from a similar position. Later, they met a shepherd who led them along a rough track and across a steep bank of scree; it was almost a sheer drop. If Alison had come this way, thought her father, she wouldn't have stood a chance. He noticed two places at which a falling person might be stopped by bushes. But it was too dangerous to investigate and they decided to turn back. At the police station they had tea before driving the ten miles to Baltal, a small village at the foot of the Zoji La pass. Nearby the river from the Amarnath glacier meets the Indus and during the annual pilgrimage to the Amarnath Cave, food and provisions are sold from tents erected in the meadows.

Kenny didn't like the look of Baltal. He instinctively held back from the sheer drop on one side of the road, but could still see the wreck of a bus that went over with 35 people on board three years earlier.

From Baltal they followed the road as it zig-zagged up the hill and arrived, a few minutes later, at an army camp. Two officers and some men gathered round to look at the photograph of Alison but weren't able to help. They had tea and Kenny looked around at the inhospitable terrain that surrounded him. No wonder the Russians are getting nowhere in Afghanistan, he thought. Might Alison have been kidnapped and left out there for dead? He asked an officer. No, came the answer, military training took place there every day and a body couldn't remain undiscovered for long.

It was dark when they got back to Sonamarg. That evening, after supper of rice and vegetable curry, he wrote in his diary:

> Doesn't anyone know it's Alison who's lost – not just any person but Alison, my Alison. What a great pal of mine, she was so nice. I know she had had moods when she was younger but she knew about that and fought against them. What a great description Liz gave the police: happy, religious – deeply so, strong, no silliness; would not smoke or drink or go with any man. Very strong. Good, naturally, at judo. Och, whats the use. She's gone now. I wish, oh, I wish it was me. She had so much to offer.

That night, he slept badly. He was very depressed.

> Oh Alison, Alison, Alison.

In the days that followed the search was intensified. A detective arrived to investigate whether there was anything sinister in Alison's disappearance. He wanted to establish whether the girl had had some kind of religious experience. Might this innocent teenager have met someone who promised to help her attain a higher spiritual plane; a guru, perhaps. She wouldn't have been the first Westerner to have succumbed to India's mystical influences. The detective questioned Kenny closely and asked Liz to repeat her story. No, he concluded, Alison MacDonald was not an impressionable and gullible teenager of the type he had encountered before. She had either had an accident, or someone had abducted her.

Kenny, meanwhile, had begun to demonstrate his organisational abilities. The villagers and shopkeepers were more than keen to help in the search. They even put up a reward of Rs1,000 for information leading to Alison's recovery. Suspicions had already been aroused that Indian soldiers were to blame, and the local Kashmiri traders were not slow to volunteer for search parties. If it could be proved that the army was behind it, those seeking an independent Kashmir would have scored a notable propaganda victory.

On the third full day of the search, Kenny mustered over seventy men to carry out a thorough search of the area between the village and the glacier. They comprised herdsmen, traders, villagers and police.

Meanwhile, a plan had been devised for trying to trace the Italian couple. It had already been established that they had flown to Kashmir for a brief holiday and were now probably back in Bologna. Kenny decided that Interpol should be brought in so Ian and Liz went off to Srinagar to phone the British High Commission in Delhi to brief them on the search and to ask them to contact Reta MacDonald. She would then be responsible for passing the Italians' names and addresses on to the police and making an official request for them to be interviewed. They caught the 8.30 a.m. bus and, on arrival, went to the home of John and Catherine Ray at the mission school. Ian phoned the High Commission as arranged and, to his amazement, discovered that his wife was in the process of doing the same thing at that very moment. The coincidence enabled them to communicate directly for the first time for a week.

Rosemary Merry was also able to speak to Liz and was overjoyed to hear her daughter's voice. She thought Liz sounded tired and sad, but was bearing up well to the trauma of her friend's disappearance. Rosemary told her husband that the story had become big news in Britain. Two days earlier she had returned home from work to find two reporters waiting for her at the gate. That evening the phone hardly stopped ringing. She answered media inquiries politely, but firmly saying, only, that Alison and Elisabeth, as Liz was called at home, were sensible girls and that both were trained in the art of self-defence. Her husband and Mr MacDonald had left London three days earlier to assist in the search for Alison and to provide support for Elisabeth. That was all she knew.

The following day she had a day off from her job in Basingstoke as a diocesan social worker for one-parent families. She agreed to be interviewed at her home and several newspaper and local radio reporters arrived at different times during the day. She also told her husband that she'd been in touch several times with Reta MacDonald in Edinburgh. Reta sounded brave and composed and was in regular contact with the Foreign Office. That afternoon Ian and Liz went to Srinagar's main post office. There they collected from poste restante a letter to Liz from her mother. It had been written before Alison disappeared and included a request for the MacDonalds' address. Little did she know she'd learn their address a few days later from a telegram.

Later that day, Liz and her father had a small get-together with the Rays and two of the school's teaching staff. It was relaxing and they enjoyed the break. They returned to Sonamarg the following day.

Kenny, meanwhile, was continuing the search of the glacier area. This time he and a party of 23 volunteers climbed higher, probing crevasses and looking behind rocks. But they had nothing to show for another day's hard graft.

Up to this point the search had concentrated on areas where Kenny thought his daughter would have gone, had she set out for a short walk. The one place in the immediate vicinity of the village where they hadn't looked was the army post on the road north. There a dozen or so soldiers of the Signals Corps were engaged in year-round monitoring duties.

The base was officially designated a 'restricted area' and it was several days before they got permission to enter. When they eventually carried out their search the police stayed well away, another symptom of their strained relationship with the military.

With the officers staying discreetly in the background, a thorough search was made of the buildings and the latrine tank was checked but, again, without success.

After ten days in Kashmir Ian decided to return home, leaving Liz and Kenny to continue the search. On the way back he reflected on his unexpected stay in India. He thought of the Hampsons who had booked him onto a flight from Delhi to London. It was another example of their unfailing kindness; of the Rays whose moral support was invaluable and of the sympathy and practical help provided by the villagers of Sonamarg. But most of all he thought of his daughter and of Kenny MacDonald. Not once had the trainee minister given in to grief, let alone despair. Outwardly he was always in good heart and his remarkable energy enabled him to maintain an almost continuously high level of activity.

Of Liz, he felt particularly proud. She had always been out in front in the search parties and showed considerable qualities of leadership. It was her staunchness in the face of adversity that made him feel something positive had emerged from this sad time in her life.

On the day that Ian Merry left Sonamarg, Kenny climbed to a height of 11,500 feet and wrote out the name ALISON in rocks on the mountain top. He had been searching, virtually non-stop, for ten days and his diary for Saturday 5 September records only that he was 'very low'. A new approach was needed. The following day he took a taxi to Srinagar. He met John Ray and was given a telegram from Reta in Edinburgh. It said: '. . . plenty of money available. Stay as long as necessary. Love Reta.' It was a great boost to his flagging morale. He now knew that the donations which started coming in so spontaneously two Sundays earlier had grown to a sizeable amount of money, several thousand pounds. He now had the means to offer a reward for information about Alison. It was, he thought, a significant development.

That day he and John Ray attended the local Church of North India, the same one Alison and Liz had worshipped in exactly four weeks earlier. In the afternoon they made a return visit to the residence of the Governor, and were introduced to his wife. Kenny told the Governor that a fund had been started in Scotland to help in the search for Alison and he was considering offering a reward. The Governor agreed it was a good idea and the following day Kenny announced through the media that Rs100,000, about £6,000, would be paid for information leading to the safe return of his daughter. For her body a sum of Rs50,000 would be paid. His strategy now was to get as much publicity as possible. He appeared on All-India television and gave interviews to radio and newspaper correspondents. Suddenly what had previously been a purely local matter was now big news. His new high-profile approach didn't take long to work. He succeeded in getting an interview with the Director-General of Police and, to his surprise, was asked what additional resources he needed.

"Fifty men, dogs and a helicopter," he said, expecting to be turned down flat.

"I'll give you 100 men and we'll see what we can do about dogs. But I'm afraid we don't have any helicopters. Only the military use them."

Before leaving police headquarters he was introduced to the man who was taking over the investigation, assistant superintendent (crime) Javed Machdoomi. The two men were to work closely together and develop a strong respect for each other.

The same day Kenny also persuaded the authorities to make armed forest rangers available. If Alison had been attacked by a wild animal, possibly a bear, or held captive by herdsmen somewhere in the mountains, the rangers' knowledge of the area could prove crucial.

Throughout his one-man blitz of officialdom, he continued to ask questions about the military. How often, and when, did the army convoys stop at Sonamarg? During their stops in the village did the soldiers wander, freely, around the shops and tea stalls?

There was not one shred of evidence that troops had been responsible for Alison's disappearance. But the fact that large numbers were in the area at the time made them prime suspects. So when he went to see the army's top brass – the chief of staff and a commander – he didn't know how they would react to his forthright questioning. There had already been suggestions of a cover-up and he expected to find the two men on the defensive, unwilling to get their soldiers embroiled any further in this potentially embarrassing case.

In fact, the two most senior officers in Kashmir were not only sympathetic, but were ready to offer whatever practical help they could. And when he left their office he had been promised that a platoon of thirty armed men would be joining the search right away.

By the time he returned to the mission school he had left the authorities in no doubt that he wanted action; no longer were half-a-dozen constables enough.

That evening, as he reflected on a day of successful badgering and cajoling, he played badminton with the Rays' daughter, Marion, and planned his next move.

Early the next morning he and Liz caught the bus back to Sonamarg. Not for the first time Liz was suffering from an upset tummy, but she had recovered enough to take part the following day in the biggest search for a missing person ever seen in Kashmir.

The police were now present in force and had established a camp at the edge of the village. They were armed and seemed well equipped for the task ahead of them.

An army major appeared in the village and asked to speak to Kenny. He was from the High Altitude Warfare School (HAWS) a few miles north of Sonamarg and wanted to know what assistance he could provide.

Twenty minutes later he had returned with ten soldiers trained to move quickly and efficiently over the most hostile terrain. They were wearing full rock-climbing kit and carrying ropes and crampons.

That morning almost two hundred police, troops and civilians formed a human chain along the base of the mountain to begin the long, systematic climb to the top.

With them was Robin, winner of the All-India police dog trials. The dog was given an article of Alison's clothing for scent and almost immediately it appeared to be on to something, heading on two separate occasions to a tourist bungalow a couple of hundred yards from the village. At the time of Alison's disappearance the bungalow was occupied by a Welsh couple and a friend. All three had since left. The dog's interest in the bungalow might have had some significance had it not, on two or more occasions, also headed straight for Liz. From this it was deduced that to Robin one European smelled much the same as another, and so its usefulness in the search was brought into question.

Nevertheless Kenny made a mental note to check out the Welsh couple and their friend.

It was an exhausting day's walking. Kenny had asked for, and got, fit, young volunteers but still reached the summit before anyone else.

They had scoured almost every square foot of the area up to and beyond the glacier, probing with sticks places where a body might be concealed. The men from the HAWS base abseiled the steep rock face of the gorge, paying particular attention to the bushes that could have broken a fall. Some of the searchers also formed an extended line to wade through the shallow lake whose murky water had been superficially investigated some days before.

But still there was no sign of Alison's body.

Kenny was certain that if she had come this way, any evidence of it had been removed. It was possible that she had fallen or been thrown into the turbulent waters of the Sindh and that her body was trapped under a rock. But the river, although at its highest, was not deep and it was thought that a body would be carried downstream by the strong current and trapped by the filters designed to stop the progress of fallen branches and other debris.

Several times the filters were investigated, but again without success.

Two days after the big sweep Kenny informed Machdoomi that he had finished searching and intended pursuing other lines of inquiry, returning first to Edinburgh to find out whether Interpol had traced the Italians.

That evening he soaked his feet in a basin of water and washed four handkerchiefs realising, too late, that there wasn't much point in the latter since he would soon be home.

The next morning he was again up early, but this time to thank the hundred or so police, traders and villagers who had gathered, as usual, to take part in the search. Then he collected Alison's belongings and he and Liz got a lift in a truck to Srinagar. That evening he took the Rays and Liz out for a meal to one of the Chinese-Tibetan restaurants on The Boulevard and enjoyed it immensely after the plain, mainly vegetarian, curries he had lived on in Sonamarg.

The next day they flew to Delhi and were met at the airport by Stephen Hampson who had booked them on a Pan Am flight to London leaving at 0545 the following morning.

Kenny had searched for his daughter virtually every day for three weeks and had come up with nothing. He didn't know whether she was alive or dead, but already he was beginning to suspect there might be more to the case than at first appeared. If she had met with an accident, why had a body not been found; not even a piece of torn clothing?

What had he established so far?

He knew from her diary that she had already been for a walk the day before she disappeared.

Liz went off to Kolahoi on horse. Went for a stroll and cut my hair. Quite a lot of tourists and army. But still beautiful – despite Italians.

He knew also that on the morning of her disappearance she had taken an early breakfast, chatted to the Italian couple staying in the next room and asked if they felt like joining her for a

63

walk on the hill opposite. He knew that at about 10 a.m. she went to the fruit stall on the opposite side of the street and bought three apples. What happened after that was a mystery. Did she cross the river to the hill opposite as planned? Did she change her mind and turn off before the bridge and head towards the gorge? Or did something happen which caused her to go in neither direction?

Although he did not yet know the answers to these questions he felt more confident of finding his daughter alive than when he first arrived in India. Yet, as he prepared to return to Edinburgh, he was affected by an overwhelming sense of sadness. He had watched police search through Alison's personal belongings and he remembered feeling momentarily outraged at this necessary indignity. He recalled, too, the pain of having to tell people that his daughter was a Christian and that she would not, under any circumstances, have gone off with someone she took a fancy to.

But now he and Liz were returning home and he felt that in a way he was deserting his daughter. If she was still alive she would be in a strange country without friend or relative. It troubled him to think that she was now all alone. His only consolation was the knowledge that although he was on his way home, his search was only just beginning.

## 7

Leopoldo Busi and Simonetta Marianucci were not typical of
Kashmir's growing number of tourists. Europeans on holiday
there usually fall into one of two quite different categories: one
group is middle-aged, well-off, and on a whistle-stop package
tour of India that takes in the best hotels in Delhi, Jaipur,
Agra and the most sumptious house boats on the Dal Lake.
The other group is young, mostly hard-up and itinerant.

The Italians fell into neither category.

They had flown to Delhi and then straight on to Srinagar
where they caught the bus to Sonamarg. All they wanted to do
during their brief summer holiday was to relax in the warm,
mountain air and perhaps do a little walking, but nothing too
strenuous. It didn't matter very much where they stayed as
long as it was cheap.

The Glacier Guest House, overlooking the Sindh and
surrounded by high, steep-sided mountains, suited them well.
Leopoldo Busi, in his early forties and separated from his
wife, enjoyed the idea of spending two weeks doing nothing.
His 35-year-old girlfriend, Simonetta Marianucci, also liked the
place and had it not been for her toothache, the holiday would
have been perfect.

They lived together in the Via Del Lavoro district of Bologna
and it was there that Kenny MacDonald found them a few
days after returning from India.

Interviewing the couple had not been part of his plan.
When he got back to Edinburgh he had expected to hear that
Interpol had done the job for him. He had hoped, simply, to
see a transcript of their story to find out if they knew which
direction Alison had taken when she left the guest house a
month earlier. But when he got home he discovered, to his
frustration and disappointment, that there was no news from
Interpol. Was he to wait until word came back from the Italian
police or start making enquires of his own? He chose to do
the latter.

Two days after his return, he and Professor Donald MacLeod
from Free Church College, went to see Chief Superintendent

Brian Cunningham of Lothian and Borders Police. It was he who had contacted Interpol after Reta MacDonald had received the names and addresses of the Italians from the Foreign Office. Kenny wanted to know why it was taking so long to trace them.

The following day Cunningham contacted Kenny to tell him he'd just received word from Interpol. The message read: 'No such people at this address; no such name in that locality.' Kenny was puzzled. Had the couple written false names and addresses in the guest house register? He could think of no reason why they should and doubts crept into his mind about the reliability of Interpol.

He phoned his friend, Alastair Ross, minister of Buccleuch and Greyfriars Free Church for advice. He happened to know the name of the minister who was the Church of Scotland's representative in Rome. His telephone number was obtained from the Church of Scotland offices in George Street, Edinburgh. Kenny rang him.

"Could you look up the Bologna phone book to see if there's anyone in the Via Del Lavoro district under Busi or Marianucci," he asked.

It turned out there were lots of them.

Round the corner from the MacDonald's flat in Marchmont was a cafe run by a friendly Italian known to everyone as Caesar. Kenny wanted to make absolutely sure he was on the right track so he asked Caesar if he would phone Bologna to check the address. Caesar obliged and was able to confirm what the minister in Rome had said regarding the number of surnames.

The same evening Kenny was on his way to Italy. He flew to London and the following morning caught a flight to Rome where he changed planes for Bologna. Within an hour of arriving there he had found the couple who might be able to unravel the mystery of Alison's disappearance.

He had traced them without any difficulty. Why, he wondered, did Interpol draw a blank in their inquiry? The only reason he could think of was that the address passed on to the Italian police turned out to be that of Simonetta's mother. But it seemed to him to be an inadequate explanation and it did nothing to lessen his misgivings about the dependability of Interpol.

The couple told him they had spoken to Alison and Liz when they arrived in Sonamarg on the Saturday. That evening Alison appeared to be 'very, very happy'. Her only worry was having caught too much sun on her face. After Liz had left for the glacier, the three talked about going for a walk on the Monday. That morning, after an early breakfast, Alison went for a brief stroll around the village, returning a short time later to find out if the others were still keen on joining her. In fact, Simonetta was suffering from toothache so they decided to postpone the walk until the following day by which time the Italian girl might be feeling better. Alison seemed satisfied with the arrangement and said she would see them later.

The Italians also told Kenny that Alison had not headed towards the gorge. Instead she walked in the direction of the bridge, apparently intent on going to the flat pasture facing the guest house on the opposite side of the river. Leopoldo was relaxing in a chair on the parched ground in front of the verandah and had expected to see her but she never appeared. Kenny regarded this information as vital. If what he had just been told was correct, she had probably intended to walk for a while before stopping at a quiet spot, away from the clamour of the village, to write home. He knew his daughter well, her likes and dislikes, and this was the type of walk he would have expected her to choose if she were on her own.

In one way he felt relieved that she had not, after all, headed towards the gorge, with its treacherous, twisting trail high above the river. But why hadn't Leopoldo, or anyone else for that matter, spotted her on the meadow opposite? The meadow is at the foot of a featureless hill of scree and rocks and Kenny thought that even in the unlikely event of her climbing a little higher someone would have seen her.

He came to the conclusion that almost certainly she never reached the meadow.

Now, for the first time, he had an eye-witness account of his daughter's movements immediately after leaving the guest house. But what he was told next was even more important.

The Italian couple and Alison were not the only people staying in the frugal, two-bedroomed, accommodation on the night of 16 August. A Kashmiri, who described himself as a businessman, was also present.

Kenny's heart was racing as the Italians told him that the man, whose name they did not know, arrived by bus from Sonamarg, the same day as Liz and Alison and left the day Alison disappeared. He had spent the two nights, Saturday and Sunday, sleeping on the floor of the Italians' room.

On the second evening Alison joined them for a meal in the small dining area adjacent to the two bedrooms. There was a discussion, lively but never heated, between Alison and the Kashmiri about religion with the man, a Muslim, arguing that Muslims and Christians had a lot in common because they both worshipped God. Alison, however, denied that that was any meaningful connection between the two faiths on the grounds that Muslims did not accept Christ as the Son of God. Later Alison returned to her own room next door.

The information about the fourth person gave a new and potentially sinister slant to the inquiry. Could this 'businessman' have followed the two girls from Srinagar, perhaps travelling on the same bus, and then, realising that one of them was alone, waited for the opportunity to strike? During the three weeks Kenny had spent in Kashmir, there had been no mention of another person staying in the guest house at the same time. He supposed the police were unaware of it, but surely the guest house owner, whom he had interviewed several times, would have known? If so, why did he keep quiet?

Kenny established from the Italians that the man was fairly young, probably in his late twenties, and unmarried. He was in business in Srinagar, exporting papier maché ornaments to cities all over Europe including, coincidentally, Bologna. He also learned that the man suffered badly from asthma and that he was associated, in some way, with a football club in Srinagar.

Kenny spent only one evening with the Italians but it was long enough to convince him, if he needed convincing, that Alison had not simply got lost in the mountains or been washed away by the river. Someone had had a hand in her disappearance and the mystery fourth person in the hotel might have played a part in it.

From the Italians, he had got a good description of the man and much additional information. As an exporter, his name would almost certainly be registered with the authorities in Srinagar. He was confident he would be able to find him. The following day Kenny was back home, preparing for his next trip to Kashmir.

For a month media interest in the case had been intense. Now, for the first time, he had to play the cat and mouse game that was to become an occasional feature of his dealings with reporters. He needed the press on his side to keep the pressure on the authorities in India during his absence. At the same time he couldn't divulge information that might tip off Alison's captors.

He decided, therefore, not to tell the press about his visit to Bologna or about his return visit to India.

Four days later, Kenny MacDonald was on his way to find the mystery man at the guest house. With him on Air India flight 108 from Heathrow was his wife, Reta, who had brought with her a set of Alison's clothes, including her tartan skirt. They arrived in Delhi at ten minutes past midnight on 26 September and were met at the airport by Mary McLaren from the British High Commission. A taxi took them to the elegant, and expensive, Akbar Hotel from where they phoned their sons, Sam and Derek, at home in Edinburgh. Kenny was also able to reimburse Miss McLaren with the money she had spent on Liz Merry's ticket home a week earlier.

After breakfast they took a taxi to the airport for the flight north to Srinagar. Over the public address system Kenny heard his name being called. One of the Indian dailies had heard that Alison MacDonald's father was on his way back to Kashmir and a reporter had been dispatched to the airport to find him. Anonymity was important to Kenny so he did not respond but he thought his cover was blown when he found the instigator of the message standing next to him.

"I am looking for Mr MacDonald but he does not seem to be answering," lamented the reporter. Kenny sympathised with the disillusioned chap but did nothing to enlighten him!

In Srinagar they took a taxi to the Tyndale Biscoe School where John Ray and his wife were introduced to Reta. Kenny told them about the fourth person at the guest house and they discussed whether or not the police should be informed. Kenny was by no means certain it was a good idea. By now he was becoming suspicious of everyone. It was possible that the police already knew about the mystery man and, for reasons best known to themselves, had done nothing about it. It was decided to seek the advice of the Governor, with whom he had established a good relationship during his previous visit.

"Can we trust the police?" he asked.

The Governor's advice was unequivocal. "Go and see Superintendent Machdoomi and tell him everything you know. He is a respected man from a respected family. You can trust him."

Meanwhile, new information emerged about the mystery man. Rosemary Merry phoned the Rays' home to tell Kenny that Liz had recognised the description given by the Italian couple. It matched that of the man who had taken the girls for a beer in Jammu, the same man who later started talking about pornographic films. Liz remembered that he had described himself as the son of a police officer.

Kenny went to see Javed Machdoomi to tell him about this startling new development. From the description, Machdoomi thought the man could be the same person he had arrested some time before for pimping.

Events were beginning to support Kenny's worst fears: that someone had spied on the girls, perhaps for two weeks or more, and then followed them to Sonamarg where his evil waiting game was unexpectedly rewarded when one of the girls was left on her own.

Machdoomi decided that Mr Watali, the Director-General of Police should be informed and he and Kenny went to his office. Watali was in a meeting but within minutes of Kenny having passed in a note bearing his name, the head of the Kashmir & Jammu police had come out to see him. Watali acted quickly and decisively. He told his subordinate to drop everything else and to work exclusively on the Alison MacDonald case. Machdoomi's first move was to radio a message to the local inspector in Sonamarg, Maharaj Machama, to arrest the owner of the guest house and have him and the house boy brought to Srinagar immediately for questioning.

In his diary, Kenny wrote: "Thank Thee Lord, things are moving'.

The investigation now concentrated on establishing whether the man at Jammu and the mystery guest at Sonamarg were one and the same. If he were, the case might soon be solved. The houseboy was released after a few days but the owner was detained in Srinagar's less than salubrious police cells for three weeks. Why, the police wanted to know, did the owner not tell them about the other man? What did he have to hide?

The police discovered that the guest house owner did have something to hide but only his failure to keep an up-to-date register. He had recorded neither the girls' names nor that of the man in the Italians' room. This was an offence under state law and he knew he faced a fine, even imprisonment, if found out. It was for this reason that he kept quiet, first about Alison's failure to return on the Monday night and later about the Kashmiri businessman.

During the owner's detention, press interest in the case intensified. Word leaked out that the hotel owner had been arrested, leading to speculation in the Indian and British media that it might lead to charges being made. But eventually the police seemed satisfied that the hapless fellow was not caught up in a plot to kidnap Alison and let him go.

The one significant fact to emerge during this period was the name of the mystery man. He was Aslem Beg, the man the Italians knew only as the papier maché exporter.

Beg was currently in Delhi on business. On the night of his return to Srinagar the police called at his home and took him away for questioning. It didn't take them long, however, to conclude that he was not the man who had made lascivious remarks to the girls in Jammu, so the theory that they and Kenny had been banking on collapsed. Nevertheless Beg's story had to be checked out. Why did he come, alone, to Sonamarg the same day as the girls, and return to Srinagar two days later?

Kenny went to interview him but didn't say who he was. The Italians had said the mystery man, now identified as Beg, knocked on Alison's door on the morning of 17 August in order to wake her up. But this conflicted with the house boy's version of events. He said Alison was up long before the others. Now Kenny wanted to establish the truth.

"Did you knock on her door?" he asked Beg.

"No," came the reply. "She was already up. She had been for a short walk and had returned. Later, while having tea, she asked if we wanted to join her."

Beg's English was good and over the next few days Kenny met him on several occasions, each time at the home of his wealthy parents, with whom he lived.

Kenny established that Beg had had a row with his father over a business matter and decided to go to Sonamarg for a couple of days to get away from it all. He said he met Alison on the Sunday night and found her to be an interesting girl. They talked about religion.

Beg's story corroborated the Italians' account in almost every detail. The only point in dispute was whether or not he had knocked on Alison's door, something he denied vehemently. His interrogator didn't let up. He wanted to be absolutely sure that Beg was in the clear. He talked to his parents about their invalid son, visited their business premises and found out as much as he could about the family.

Beg's asthma was chronic. Kenny felt that even if this was the kidnapper, he would have been no match for Alison, a green belt in judo.

There remained the possibility that Beg may have been part of a gang, his role being to spy on the girl and tip off a third party about her movements. But Kenny had probed and questioned relentlessly and was as sure as he possibly could be that Aslem Beg was not responsible for his daughter's disappearance. Two days earlier he felt close to solving the mystery; now he was back at square one.

Until now the reward for Alison's safe recovery had stood at Rs100,000, about £6,000. The reward had attracted much press coverage but little in the way of hard facts. Now the MacDonalds faced a new dilemma. Should they increase it substantially in the hope that greed might persuade someone to talk?

It was a difficult decision. For one thing the fund, at the Clydesdale Bank in Stornoway, stood at just a few thousand pounds, far less than they proposed to offer. Secondly, their strength during the previous five agonising weeks had been drawn from their unwavering Christian faith. If God had intended

Alison to be returned to them, He would do so, whatever material incentives they dangled before the people of Kashmir.

John Ray was brought into the discussion and the three agreed to increase the reward to 3 *lakh*, one *lakh* being Rs100,000. That meant the MacDonalds had to be prepared to pay out £18,000 and the only way they could do that was to sell their flat in Edinburgh if necessary.

Dozens of photographs of Alison were printed, ready for distribution to newspapers, television and police stations. But for the time being it was decided to say nothing about the new reward.

Ever since Aslem Beg's elimination from the police inquiry, the trail had gone cold. But on 5 October Kenny got a phone call from Superintendent Machdoomi about a potentially significant new development. Machdoomi had received a tip-off from an informer that a taxi had arrived at the Glacier Guest House at 9 p.m. on 17 August, the day of Alison's disappearance. The vehicle left four hours later at 1 a.m.; it had come from the small town of Kangan mid-way between Srinagar and Sonamarg and was said to be owned by the same man who owned the guest house.

Once again, the spotlight was on the person who had earlier concealed information from the police.

The information was important because the taxi could have been used to smuggle Alison out of Sonamarg under the cover of darkness.

The taxi driver was traced by the police and the guest house owner was again interrogated. Both confirmed the taxi story but with one important difference – it happened three days earlier on 14 August.

The informer's story was checked and checked again, this time by Kenny. He went to the taxi driver's home and got him to state, once more, the exact date and time he was in Sonamarg. Finally he accepted that the taxi driver was telling the truth and that the informer had got his dates mixed up. Whether he had done so deliberately or otherwise was never established. Once again, the inquiry had stumbled on stony ground.

The Macdonalds began to dispair. They felt that the investigation was getting nowhere. Kenny and Reta killed time, wondering what to do next. They went shopping in the Government handicraft emporiums and strolled along the Bund, the tree-lined footpath by the side of the Jhelum River. Reta bought herself a pair of boots.

One evening *The Times*'s correspondent in Delhi phoned. He wanted to know about the man arrested by police. The next day there were more calls from the media, each seeking confirmation of *The Times*'s story. Two BBC local radio stations in Scotland, Radio Highland and the Gaelic station, also rang.

What they didn't know at that stage was that the man in question, Aslem Beg, had been questioned and released several days earlier. He had been detained only for one night.

Reta MacDonald felt unexpectedly at ease when she stepped off the bus next to Sonamarg's biggest and best stocked craft shop. It was her first visit to the place from which her daughter had disappeared eight weeks earlier and she was unsure how her emotions would stand up to it. Sonamarg had been described as a tawdry, even ugly, place, but on the contrary she felt reassured by the beauty of the valley. It was not, as she had imagined, an inhospitable outpost on the road to nowhere. Instead she found a village, not threatening or ominous but agreeable, even enticing. Like her husband before, she felt this was a place in which Alison would have been at peace. If she had any misgivings about the village it was the shopkeepers whom she regarded with some suspicion.

That night they stayed in Alison's room at the Glacier Guest House. It was dark by half past six and a lantern and candles provided the only light for reading. They went to bed at 9.30 p.m. but neither of them slept well.

Next morning they set off to cover as much ground as possible. First they surveyed the hill opposite and later walked part of the way up the river, checking the gully that looked so menacing.

They also called at the military base used by the handful of men of the Signals Corps and had tea and cakes with the officers.

Later, as they continued to explore the immediate vicinity of the village, they tried to imagine which route Alison might have taken. Kenny had investigated the area many times before but he wanted Reta to see it also. Perhaps her reading of the situation would be different from his.

They chose to climb the Luderwas, the 12,000-feet peak that rose steeply from the meadow opposite the guest house.

It was a long, exhausting haul, but they reached the top and were rewarded with a breath-taking view of the valley. Round about were half-eaten conifer cones, a reminder that this was bear country.

Kenny's legs had been toughened and his lungs expanded by hours of slogging some weeks earlier. For Reta it was a new and arduous experience but it proved, not that it needed proof, that her resolve was undiminished.

It had been a nerve-wracking climb over scree and rocks and through thorny bushes. Now it was getting late and their fatigue had given way to outright fear of being stranded on the mountain overnight. On the top they read from the Bible they had brought with them and prayed for their safe return to the village.

On one side there was a sheer drop and each time they searched for a way down they were faced with the same obstacle. The light began to fade and they considered lighting a fire in the hope that someone in the village would see it. But just as it looked as though they would have to stay put until morning, they found a gully they could negotiate safely and were able to clamber down, a task made easier by the near full moon whose reflection on the river below illuminated the bank like a beacon.

They eventually reached the river at ten past six by which time it was almost dark.

It had been a frightening experience. They were never in any real danger of falling, but at night the temperature on the highest peaks falls to below zero and they had neither sleeping bags, nor warm clothing.

It was not beyond the bounds of possibility that the mountain which might have claimed Alison could so easily have also killed her parents. The point was not lost, either, on the man put in charge of the Glacier Guest House during the owner's detention in Srinagar. With his boss still suspected of complicity in Alison's disappearance he had been to the police station no fewer than three times to report that now her parents were also missing. He was a relieved man when they turned up safe and well.

The following day the MacDonalds returned to Srinagar, having spent the morning scouring the area below the Thajiwas Glacier from the back of hired ponies. In their absence, John Ray had done his best to fend off the many reporters who called or phoned but there was no further news from Machdoomi and, in spite of the reward, no one had come forward with information. That night Kenny wrote in his diary:

> Looked through Alison's books etc. Pain, pain, pain. I'm sure my heart will not stand it. Reta low as well.

The three men who turned up at the Ray's home at 5 p.m. on 12 October were quite open about why they wanted to meet Kenny MacDonald: they were interested in the reward.

Their spokesman was Ghulam Nabi, a startlingly handsome man of about 26 with dark, flashing eyes. Nabi was confident, had a good command of English, and put their case well. He said they had read in the papers that a reward would be paid for the safe return of Alison MacDonald. They didn't know where she was but their knowledge of the area was such that they could find her.

The reward, at this point, stood at only 1 *lakh* (Rs100,000). It was still a sizeable amount of money, but far short of the 3 *lakh* reward that hadn't yet been made public. Two of the men, Nabi and Amin Chapri were known to John Ray. They were both old boys of his school and Chapri was an accomplished trekking guide whose family owned many of the biggest and best houseboats on the lake. The family was not without money. Chapri had been, and perhaps still was, involved in the Kashmir Liberation Front and knew many of the mountain passes that separate Kashmir and Pakistan. The third man was Muhammed Yagub, about whom John Ray knew nothing.

Nabi, ice cool and immaculately dressed, spelled out what they wanted: an advance now, the rest when they produced Alison.

By their own admision they were bounty hunters. But their frankness appealed to Kenny who sensed that they might indeed, know something.

He didn't agree to their terms but told them the money was theirs when they produced Alison.

The three men had done their homework. They produced pages of notes and newspaper cuttings on the case. Chapri's knowledge of the mountains was considerable and this, coupled with the brains of Nabi meant they could not be dismissed as malevolent time wasters.

Whether malevolence would manifest itself in other ways remained to be seen.

The MacDonalds had planned to return to Scotland on 16 October, but the approach from the three men caused them to delay their journey home.

After the disappointments of their eighteen-day stay in Kashmir, the couple were emotionally drained. The physical search of Sonamarg had provided no clues whatsoever and now the police inquiry was being scaled down. Machdoomi was transferred to the traffic division and although his interest in the case remained, he had litle time to devote to it.

What Nabi and his friends had done was to provide the MacDonalds with new hope. They realised they might be the victims of a cruel hoax but felt they had no choice but to go along with these enigmatic characters.

Kenny knew that Nabi, whom he had dubbed 'the cobra' because of his quick tongue was no fool. He didn't trust him but neither could he afford to ignore him. No further meeting had been arranged and all he could do now was wait.

He and Reta tried to relax. They played badminton together and went for long walks. They took an auto-rickshaw along the Boulevard and at the landing stage opposite Nehru Park, they bargained with the shikari boys for the price of an hour or two on the lake. In the still, watery glades of the floating gardens the boat prised a path through the lilies that spread before them like a mermaid's dinner service and in the lovely tranquility of the backwaters of the Dal Lake they prayed that their heartache would soon be over.

The next day a group of young Indian missionaries came to see the MacDonalds at the Rays' home. The missionaries, from Mizoram close to the border with Burma, had been in Kashmir for some time distributing Christian literature. They knew about the missing daughter of the Scots trainee minister and had been making their own inquiries during their travels. Now they had come to report the sighting of a white girl at the village of Narannag, about 30 kms from Sonamarg. They had seen, in a guest house register, a foreign name alongside those of five Kashmiri men and when they checked with the owner he confirmed the name was that of an European woman.

This in itself was important but what particularly interested Kenny was not the name of the woman, which might have been false, but that of one of the five men. He was called Ibrahim Chapri, the brother of Amin, the tourist guide who had called at the mission school days earlier with his two colleagues. It was arguably the most significant development in the case so far.

The following day the MacDonalds received another visit from Chapri, Nabi and Yagub whom the couple now referred to as the 'three musketeers'. Nabi said they had consulted an astrologer who claimed to have 'seen' Alison sitting in a chair reading a book. By her side were two dogs, one of them black and white.

In fact Alison did have two dogs; her own dog, Lady, and the family pet, Glen. Both were black-and-white collies. She was also in the habit of spending hours in a chair reading. Their description of the girl was vague. Nevertheless it was sufficiently accurate to leave the MacDonalds in a state of bewilderment. Not for one moment did they believe the story about the astrologer but they began to wonder whether their visitors knew more about the case than they were prepared to admit. Kenny continued trying to prise more information out of them but they insisted that they knew only what the astrologer had told them.

However, they were sure of one thing: Alison was alive and well and being held prisoner not very far away. They were unable or unwilling to say where, or by whom, but they could find out and would bring her back.

Then they spelled out their terms. They wanted Rs100,000 delivered in 24 hours. On receipt of the money, one parent would be told where Alison could be collected.

Kenny and Reta were certain they had become entwined in a web of lies but decided to meet their visitors' demands. An agreement was drawn up by John Ray, whom the men said they trusted, and the MacDonalds said they would have the reward money as soon as they could lay their hands on it.

The couple felt that at long last they knew what had happened to their daughter. She had been kidnapped and was being held hostage until a ransom was paid. They had no idea whether the 'three musketeers' were the kidnappers, intermediaries acting on behalf of the kidnappers, or genuine bounty hunters. But of one thing they were quite sure: their daughter was alive and there was now a real chance that their nightmare was about to end. They realised that things could still go wrong but if they came up with the money there was a real chance that they, together with Alison, could soon be leaving Kashmir forever.

That night, Kenny wrote in his diary:

She must be alive and Cobra knows where she is. Parent only to collect her: reward in 24 hours. This must be it.

And later, as he tossed and turned in bed:

Can't sleep – excited. Lord keep her safe till we get her.

The MacDonalds had a lot to do in Delhi and not much time in which to do it.

First, they went to see Mary McLaren at the High Commission but she held out little hope of getting Rs100,000 by the following day and the accountant whose advice had been sought, agreed.

"But we've got to get the money," said Kenny.

"Well in that case let's try," said Miss McLaren.

They went to her personal bank, Grindlays, and were shown into the manager's office.

"We need one *lakh*," said Kenny, after explaining the circumstances. "Can you help?"

"Certainly," came the reply from behind the huge leather-topped desk. "How soon do you need the cash?"

Kenny said he needed it right away.

The manager called an assistant to find out what was the highest denomination of notes they had in the bank and decided that the parcel would be too big to carry back to Srinagar safely. Even if the MacDonalds avoided getting mugged in the heaving streets of New Delhi they would have a monumental problem explaining their bag of money to security staff at the airport.

The manager said he'd phone the branch of Grindlays in Srinagar and make arrangements for the cash to be delivered to the Rays' home the following day.

The financial business over, the manager rang for tea. "Now tell me, where in Scotland are you from?" he enquired.

"We live in Edinburgh," said Reta, "but my husband is from Skye and I come from Orkney."

"Now there's a coincidence. I thought I detected an Orcadian accent there. I'm from Westray, myself."

Not only had they got the money without any difficulty, they also discovered that the helpful Scots banker sitting opposite was a fellow islander.

They thanked the manager for his co-operation and left, promising that the money would be transferred from Scotland as soon as possible.

Miss McLaren, who was with them, suggested they then go to the local office of British Airways.

The manager, Chris Cross, listened to their story and promised to do all he could to ensure that the MacDonalds and Alison were on the 0545 London flight four days later, even though all the seats were already taken.

He accepted, without question, assurances from Kenny and Miss McLaren that the tickets would be paid for retrospectively and agreed that the three seats he booked in fictitious names. Kenny was to phone him from Srinagar to say only whether the operation was on or off. He would do the rest.

That evening Kenny and Reta took Miss McLaren out for a Chinese meal. It wasn't exactly a celebration but they felt closer than at any time since the search began to being reunited with their daughter.

All being well she would be with them on that plane in a few days time.

Later they phoned their other daughter, Mairi, who was staying at her parents' home in Edinburgh, to tell her the encouraging news. They also spoke, briefly, to Sam and Derek. Now the whole family knew that if things went to plan, Alison would be back home soon.

Meanwhile, the reward money had to be sorted out so Mairi was asked to contact the Stornoway branch of the Royal Bank of Scotland to have the equivalent of Rs100,000 transferred to Grindlays in Delhi. The Royal was handling the appeal fund set up almost two months earlier and the MacDonalds reckoned it contained enough to cover both the reward and the flights home.


The MacDonalds arrived back at the Rays in the middle of the following afternoon and, at 3 p.m. as arranged, the cash was delivered. It was contained in a plain, brown carrier bag and accompanying it in the back seat of a taxi was the manager of the local branch of Grindlays who obviously felt that such an important mission warranted his personal attention. All there was to do now was wait. It was 9 o'clock in the evening when Ghulam Nabi eventually appeared. Amin Chapri was not with him but the third man, Mahammed Yagub, was.

The MacDonalds had expected this to be the meeting at which arrangements would be finalised for the handing over of the reward money in exchange for Alison or, at the very least, definite information of her whereabouts.

Instead they were left feeling demoralised and utterly dejected. They had built up their hopes only to be told by Nabi that he needed more time, another 15 days.

They were too low in spirits to be angry. Nabi's attitude had changed completely. Previously he had been assertive and precise; now he was evasive and vague. He muttered something about the astrologer not coming up with enough information and now Kenny realised that he might have been wrong in believing this man knew where Alison was. He wondered whether the indecisive, furtive figure before him had come under pressure to change his story. Was he a middle man acting for a group of kidnappers? Or did he and the others uncover a plot which was now too hot for them to handle?

Kenny didn't know. The three might just as easily have been three rogues, hoping to cash in on a mother and father's emotional instability. Or they might genuinely have hoped to collect the reward money by finding the body of a young woman accidentally killed in the mountains.

Yet there had been too many coincidences, too many unanswered questions, for the events of the past few days to be put down to a distraught father's gullibility. Hard facts were thin on the ground but there had been enough pointers to convince both parents that someone knew something about their daughter's disappearance. And although they were now flying home without Alison they each knew they would be back soon to continue the search for her.

> Alison we are leaving today. Oh, my darling would that you were with us. Oh Alison, my darling Alison. Please God, let thy glory be revealed by returning Alison to us.

# 8

A Kashmiri winter is bitterly cold and in the valleys the deep snow provides a protective cover for the gladioli, narcissi, daffodils and a host of other plants that wait patiently for spring.

Smoke from thousands of wood stoves hangs heavily over Srinagar. The streets are a quagmire of slush and mud and the flat-topped roofs of the houseboats creak under the weight of the melting snow.

The people have an ingenious way of keeping warm. A *kangri*, an earthenware bowl in a wicker basket, is filled with hot charcoal and carried around as casually as an umbrella. Sometimes the *kangri* is held underneath a *pheran*, a woollen garment rather like a poncho, giving the impression that the wearer is either very pot-bellied or very pregnant. These personal central heating systems accompany their owners everywhere, even to bed, and there are some harrowing stories of people snuggling up to their *kangri* and getting badly burned.

For the Gujars, the Muslim herdsmen, who travel south with the advancing snowline, winter is a time for doing business. Their sheep, reared in the mountains for their wool and mutton, are sold in the markets of Srinagar and Jammu and even their cattle, sacred animals throughout the rest of India, end up on the butcher's block. Many of Kashmir's Hindus are high caste Brahims whose menfolk often adopt the name *pandit*, meaning teacher. But unlike their brethren elsewhere they do not abhor the eating of beef, preferring, instead, to eschew things like garlic and onions which they believe encourage base passions. This convenient culinary practice means that in Kashmir, Hindus may eat beef with impunity.

Even the bears abandon the mountains in winter and in villages like Sonamarg there is ample evidence of their nocturnal searches for food. But these bears seldom attack human beings and confine their fleeting raids, even in the depths of winter, to only the most isolated settlements.

So, it was a very different Kashmir that Kenny McDonald returned to in the last days of November 1981. When he and

Reta had flown home to Edinburgh six weeks earlier, their hearts heavy with sadness and disappointment, they left behind a Kashmir still mellow and soft in the red dusk of autumn. Now it was harsh and threatening and he wondered how Alison would fare, for he was certain she was still alive.

As he passed quickly through customs and immigration control at Srinagar airport he looked a strange figure. He had grown a beard and was wearing sunglasses in an effort to avoid recognition. For the first few weeks of this, his third visit to Kashmir, anonymity was essential.

His studies for the ministry in Edinburgh had been seriously disrupted by Alison's disappearance and now he had been forced to miss the end-of-term examinations. But the events of October convinced him that someone was hiding something and now it was important to keep the momentum going. He could not afford to delay his return, even by a week or two. This time he decided to stay not with the Rays who were about to make their annual visit to Scotland, but on board the houseboat *Sharin*, from where Alison and Liz Merry had enjoyed the charm of the Dal Lake during their days in Srinagar.

Staying there was not an easy decision. For one thing the vessel provided only the most basic accommodation and in the dank, reeking cold, the black water of the lake took on an even more chilling appearance.

It was also difficult, emotionally. In Sonamarg he had been vexed by the painful experience of seeing Alison's room at the guest house and going through her belongings. He remembered, too, his sense of despair, of helplessness, as the police took an item of his daughter's clothing as scent for the dog. It was this, perhaps more than anything else, that touched a nerve still numbed by that phone call only a few nights earlier. Now, on the *Sharin*, he was exposing his ravaged emotions to more torment. This was the place Alison had described in her diary as 'sublime' and now he was alone in the bed his daughter had slept in only three nights before she went missing.

Kenny had two good reasons for returning to Kashmir so soon after his last visit. First, he wanted to question Omar Bashir, the young man who befriended Alison and Liz in Srinagar. The other was to whet the media's appetite for the human interest mileage to be gained from the visit of his wife, Reta, and their two sons. And just to be absolutely sure of making the headlines he also planned to announce that the reward for Alison's safe recovery had been increased to 3 *lakh*.

Omar Bashir owned a thriving business selling locally produced handicrafts, mainly to the tourists. The girls met him on the day prior to leaving Srinagar for Sonamarg. Alison bought a cushion from him and, in the evening, he took them to the Hotel Shahenshah where they had kebabs and listened to Kashmiri music. The girls enjoyed the hospitality shown to them and unlike the last time a man took them out for a drink, in Jammu, there were no unpleasant sexual overtones. Nevertheless Kenny MacDonald was determined to follow up every possible lead, no matter how tenuous. He soon established where Bashir worked and called at his shop.

In keeping with his habit of catching suspects off guard, he did not revel his identity. But Bashir soon wakened to the fact that this was the father of the girl missing in Sonamarg and, guessing that he was under suspicion, denied any knowledge of her disappearance.

In spite of the young man's indignant protestations, Kenny was not fully satisfied that the well-off Muslim was innocent. Bashir told him that he was alone when he went to the Shahenshah with the two girls; yet Kenny knew from Liz that another man had been present. When challenged on this point, Bashir admitted that a second man was there. But to Bashir, a man of some standing, a mere driver of taxis did not count. He, the taxi driver, had sat apart from the small group and it had not occurred to Bashir that any significance would be attached to him.

Kenny accepted the explanation and put it down to one of the conventions of Kashmir's and, for that matter, India's class system. But just to be certain, he told the police about his meeting and the unfortunate taxi driver spent a day in the cells before being released.

Kenny was beginning to realise that in Kashmir there were no bounds to the wheeling and dealing that went on under the cloak of respectable business. So he asked Bashir if he could see his bank account.

It was a long shot but he wanted to be sure that Bashir had not engaged in any significant financial dealings for which he had no satisfactory explanation. Anxious to have any lingering suspicion finally lifted from him, Bashir reluctantly agreed and allowed Kenny to inspect his bank account.

Everything appeared to be in order except for one thing. Why had Bashir recently made a payment to the Chapri family? Amin Chapri was still very much under suspicion and it seemed at best a coincidence, at worst a sign of Bashir's complicity, that the Chapris should have received a not insignificant sum of money from Bashir.

Twenty-five years as a customs officer had sharpened Kenny's ability to spot a liar but now, after several weeks of questioning sometimes evasive Kashmiris his powers of interrogation had been honed to a fine edge. Using his new-found skills he was able to establish that houseboat owners who point their guests in the direction of a particular shop can expect a small backhander for their trouble. It seemed that the Chapri family had been putting business Bashir's way and the payment was their cut. It was a perfectly legitimate payment and the explanation was enough to finally convince Kenny that the man whom his daughter had met only three days before she went missing was not the man he was looking for.

Nevertheless, the bank manager didn't much care for the fact that one of his clients had been under suspicion in the Alison MacDonald case and Omar Bashir was asked to take his account elsewhere.

Kenny's unquenchable desire to find Alison meant he kept up a constantly high level of activity. He was always on the move stopping to talk to shopkeepers and making himself as visible as possible to the public. Often he would be stopped in the street and offered words of encouragement and he felt that, if ever Alison's captors were caught, they would probably suffer an unthinkable fate if the people of Srinagar got their hands on them.

With the Rays away, he returned alone to the *Sharin* every night to eat. But not even the most obliging houseboy could be expected to share such eccentric hours so he often had to cook his own meals in the ill-equipped galley, a task made all the more difficult by Srinagar's unreliable electricity supply in winter. But he persevered, causing much mirth among the houseboat wallahs with his version of a Kashmiri hot-pot: raw mutton, carrots, potatoes and any other recognisable food he could find in Srinagar's market stalls. The whole lot would then be stewed for hours in a big pot and consumed over three or more days. The resulting hash did little to endear the disbelieving onlookers to Scottish cuisine.

Life on the *Sharin* was lonely. At night as he lay in his sleeping bag trying to keep warm he read his Bible and marked passages that had a particular relevance at the time.

He also wrote home. But in a part of the world where men in uniform, even a postal clerk's uniform, are king, he thought it prudent to write in Gaelic just in case his letters were intercepted. It was a wise precaution as he discovered later that mail was frequently opened either at the general post office or by Customs officers. However the method was not without irony; not only did his letters fox the Indian authorities, they also foxed Reta who had to take them to Professor MacLeod at the Free Church offices in Edinburgh to have them translated.


On the day that Alison disappeared the Signals Corps base at Sonamarg was unusually quiet. The few military personnel stationed there had been given a long week-end off and the only people that remained were eight civilians employed by Military Engineering Services (MES).

Ever since Kenny had broken down the previously impenetrable shield the Army in Kashmir threw around itself, the police had found the military much more co-operative, at least as far as the Alison Macdonald inquiry was concerned.

As a result Superintendent Javed Machdoomi had been able to go into the base and interview the MES men to find out if they knew anything.

But one man had not been interviewed. He was a Sikh called H. K. Singh who soon after the incident had been posted to the small town of Umbala in the north Indian state of Haryana.

As Kenny was looking particularly for any irregularity in the routine of army personnel or civilians in the Sonamarg area, the posting of H. K. Singh so soon after Alison's disappearance warranted further investigation. It didn't take him long to persuade the brigadier in charge of the Sonamarg base to start proceedings to have the man brought to Srinagar for questioning.

Meanwhile, as India's bureaucracy creaked into action, Kenny continued his inquiries in Srinagar. He again went to see Aslam Beg and had further meetings with Ghulam Nabi and Amin Chapri. He also went to the village of Narannag to check the register of the guest house at which Amin Chapri's brother had stayed with some other Kashmiris and a European girl.

This lead had already been thoroughly investigated but Kenny wanted to be absolutely sure there was no connection. In the event he was able to confirm that one of the Kashmiris had studied engineering in West Germany where he had met and married a local girl. It was she whom the Christian missionaries thought might have been Alison.

Reta MacDonald was due to join her husband in mid-December. This was to be her second visit but the first for the couple's two sons, Sam (16) and Derek (11). Alison's twentieth birthday fell on December 25 and it was thought that a visit to Sonamarg on or near Christmas Day by other members of the family would attract a lot of sympathetic publicity. Only Mairi, who was expecting her second child, would be left at home.

The plan was to play on the emotions of the people of Kashmir through press and television pictures of a close-knit family whose lives had been thrown into turmoil by events four months earlier.

In the days before the arrival of Reta and the boys, Kenny prepared the ground for their visit by nurturing the media contacts he had made during previous visits. He would need them in a few days time when he announced that the reward money for Alison's safe return had been trebled.

But he felt that the reward, alone, might not be enough; what he also needed was a guarantee that whoever had kidnapped his daughter would be immune from prosecution. With this in mind he went to see the Governor, the Chief of Police and the Army's Chief of Staff and was relieved when they agreed to his suggestion of an amnesty. So far as they were concerned, Alison MacDonald was simply a missing person; if her father chose not bring charges against the person or persons responsible for her disappearance they would not overrule him.

He now felt that he had a strong card to play when Reta and the boys arrived. Firstly, there was the human interest value in the visit to Sonamarg on Alison's birthday. Then there was the fact the reward was to be increased to 3 *lakhs*, a lot of money even in the relatively wealthy state of Jammu & Kashmir. And finally there was the amnesty for her kidnappers.

Meanwhile, he continued to make himself known in the shops and bazaars. Most people seemed to know of the case of the Scots girl missing in Sonamarg and her father's relentless efforts to find her and, judging by the reactions he got, they seemed genuinely shocked that a crime of passion, if that is what it was, could happen in Kashmir. Nevertheless, someone, somewhere knew what had happened to her and his feelings, towards the Kashmiris were tempered by a suspicion of almost everyone he met. If there was one single group he felt he could trust it was the army officers who struck him as being men of integrity. The fact that a few were also Christians was another reason for accepting their word.

# 9

No sooner had the British Airways flight from Heathrow touched down at Delhi International Airport than it screeched and shuddered to an abrupt halt. Over the public address system the captain apologised to his passengers and explained that a brake failure light had come on. There would be a short delay before the aircraft could continue taxi-ing towards the terminal.

It was all Derek needed. He'd never flown further than Stornoway and Kirkwall before and he hated the clinging claustrophobic atmosphere in the aircraft after the long journey via Kuwait and Dubai. He didn't like the food, felt sick, and just wanted to go to bed, a real bed, like they have in hotels; not a reclining seat like on the plane.

But his discomfort wasn't over yet. The delay meant that when the 747 finally reached its allotted place on the apron, it disgorged its load at precisely the same time as two other Jumbos. The result was bedlam in the hot, smelly terminal building as what seemed like half the subjects of the United Nations jostled for a place in one of the two queues for immigration control.

Reta and the boys waited and waited, Derek becoming increasingly ill-looking. Then just as he looked as though he was going to keel over in the stupifying heat, Reta walked to the head of the queue, pleaded with the man at immigration to let her son through and before they knew it they were free of the heaving mass of humanity and able to breathe again. Kenny had flown down from Srinagar the day before and was at the airport to meet them. For him it was a welcome break. He had been without family or close friends for over two weeks and he was especially glad to see his wife and their two sons.

They flew on to Srinagar the same day and from the plane the boys were able to see, for the first time, the phenomenal beauty of the mountains and forests below.

But there was nothing beautiful about Srinager. The yellow smog above the city blotted out the sun that looked so strong from the plane and the cold dampness of the place seemed to seep through to their very bones.

The Rays were still on holiday in Edinburgh visiting Catherine's elderly parents and they'd offered to let the MacDonalds have the use of their home, complete with Kala the houseboy, during their absence. The offer was gratefully accepted.


After the early publicity the story of the Scots girl missing in Sonamarg had all but disappeared from the local newspapers. But the news that the reward had been increased to 3 *lakh* was to change all that. Kenny called at the offices of the two main newspapers, *Aftab* and the *Srinagar Times* and rang the correspondents of a number of other newspapers including *The Times of India* and the *Hindustan Times*. The local stringer for the *Daily Telegraph*, Mr J. N. Sathu, was also given the story.

Kenny also went on local television to say that the authorities had agreed to an amnesty for Alison's kidnappers. The reward would be paid with no questions asked.

The decision to increase the reward by so much was not taken lightly. Not only was the sum beyond his or the appeal fund's means, he was also conscious of the fact that such a large sum of money might encourage a spate of kidnappings of European women. However, he had discussed that with Reta and the Rays some weeks earlier and it had been decided to go ahead.

All he and his wife could now do was wait to see what response, if any, would result from the massive publicity. Meanwhile the efforts to have H. K. Singh brought to Srinagar for questioning had become tangled in a furlong of Indian red tape. The eighth man at the Signals base at Sonamarg was still somewhere near Delhi and the police seemed to have no appetite for putting pressure on the military authorities in whose hands the matter lay. Kenny, now with Derek and Sam for company, went to see an Army general but was fobbed off with more excuses about the delay in interviewing Singh. In fact it was to be several weeks more before the Sikh civilian was questioned about his movements in Sonamarg during the weekend of 15-17 August. Kenny despaired at the lethargy of officialdom and got on with his unrelenting search for Alison. Wherever he and the family went, he asked if anyone had seen a pretty 19-year-old European girl and guest house registers were checked in case she had stayed there.

On one occasion they all went to Gulmarg, a small village at 9,000 feet which is India's main ski-ing resort and also the site of one of the highest golf courses in the world. Vakil, who was on the teaching staff at the Tyndale Biscoe school, offered to drive them there in the elderly school truck. They left early in the morning on the 35-mile journey but it was so cold Vakil had to light a fire under the diesel tank before the engine spluttered into action.

Usually, in winter, the ski slopes of Gulmarg are dotted with Japanese, but this time the snow was thin on the ground. As a result there was little work and therefore little income for the scores of *pheren*-clad boys and men who make their living by operating the ski tows, carrying skis or acting as general dogs-bodies. This meant they were even more desperate than usual for business so when the MacDonalds climbed down from the cold and cramped cab of the battered vehicle they were besieged by an army of hawkers selling everything from tea to toboggans.

Reta disliked the place intensely. In a village on the way there she had seen crippled beggars, the first real poverty she had encountered in Kashmir, and in Gulmarg, itself, she was overcome with a feeling that varied between melancholy and pity.

Everywhere they went they were surrounded by people trying to sell them things. Kenny spoke to them in Gaelic in an effort to confuse them but still they persisted. The family was glad when Vakil decided it was time to head back.

The announcement about the reward had the desired effect. The story was still making the headlines several days later and the family were recognised wherever they went. For the boys it was a strange experience. Their thoughts were dominated by their missing sister but, apart from accompanying their father from time to time, there was little they could do so they took the opportunity of exploring the city.

The weather was miserable. The smog reminded Reta of the pea-soupers London was once famous for and she imagined that catarrh and chest infections must be common here.

For the MacDonalds, 25 December 1981 was a day for thinking more than usual about Alison. Not only was it her twentieth birthday, it was also the first Christmas she had not been at home with her parents.

On Christmas Eve, Kenny, Reta and the two boys went to the watchnight service at the Church of North India. Although it was bitterly cold, there was no breeze and all around the outside of the church candles flickered in the still night air.

Christmas dinner, the following day, was a *piece de resistance* from Kala, the Rays' long-serving houseboy, a man in his mid-forties. The day before he had summoned Reta into his kitchen to inspect the Christmas fare, two live and kicking hens, and now here they were beautifully cooked without so much as a hint of curry, much to Derek's delight. Next came apricot pudding – not quite plum pudding, but near enough.

The next morning the MacDonalds got up early. This was to be the day Sam and Derek were to see the village from which their older sister had disappeared. When the taxi arrived it was still dark but by the time they had reached Kangan, an hour and a half's drive away, the sun had penetrated the early morning mist that hung, motionless, in the valley as though frozen by the lens of a camera.

At last they had left the smokey atmosphere of Srinagar far behind. Here the air was clear and crisp and the sky was a deep blue against the white jagged peaks of the mountains. The road was heavily rutted by ice and snow and as they approached the steep, twisting section that meant they were nearing Sonamarg, the taxi skidded to a sudden halt.

"I can take you no further," said the driver, pointing to the sheet of ice that covered the road.

They arranged to meet the taxi driver five hours later at the same spot and set off on the four-mile trek to Sonamarg. Conditions underfoot made walking difficult and progress was slow.

The sun, brilliant in a cloudless sky, filled the valley but the temperature was probably minus five or colder and here, at almost 9,000 feet they were glad they had brought warm clothing.

The River Sindh, fast and menacing when Kenny had first seen it, was now silent under a heavy mantle of solid ice. Even the small waterfalls were frozen as though in a state of suspended animation.

Sam, who was later to go to art school, had brought a sketch pad and water colours with him. But the reflection of the intense sun on the white paper made it difficult to see properly and when he tried to overcome the problem by moving into the shade it was so cold he could hardly hold the brush. The road was deserted, apart from the MacDonalds and a family of Ladakhis, a man and a woman and their teenage son, some distance behind. They each had a bundle tied to their backs. The three were strung out like a polar expedition and when they reached Sonamarg they just kept going.

The weather had been less severe than usual and the village, usually cut off from November until April, showed some signs of life. Thin wisps of smoke came from a few of the wooden huts and on the lower slopes a handful of men were gathering wood. But the main part of the village, the part the tourists see, was deserted except for two men whose job it was to clear snow from the rooftops to stop them caving in under the weight. A savage-looking dog, tethered to a rope, barked loudly. Kenny had seen similar beasts during his first trip to Sonamarg. They belonged to the Gujars and he soon learned to give the dogs a wide berth.

Sam and Kenny walked up to the Signals Corps base on the other side of the bridge and noticed that it was still occupied. As they were leaving, three soliders approached them and asked where they were going and whether they had transport. In an area of great military sensitivity they were obviously being checked out.

Later, the family had tea with the two snow clearers in front of a big roaring fire in a room in the tourist centre and were subjected to tall tales about yetis. Yetis, it was claimed, had been seen in the mountains and it was possible that Alison had been carried away by one.

They also said that two months earlier two people had been murdered in Sonamarg. Kenny and Reta wondered if the story, like that of the yetis, was the product of a vivid imagination. But it soon became evident that there was nothing mythical about the double murder. According to the two men, a local tea-shop owner failed to return to Srinagar after closing down his business in Sonamarg for the winter. The alarm was raised and when police searched his boarded up premises they found not only the body of the owner but also that of his girlfriend. It was also discovered that the summer's takings had been stolen. Later, a Bengali, who worked for the owner, was arrested and charged.

The two snow clearers said these were the first murders in the village anyone could remember. There had been no history of violence and the whole community had been shocked by the occurrence.

From what the MacDonalds had just been told there seemed to be no connection whatsoever with the murders and Alison's disappearance. Nonetheless the news sent a shiver down their spines. Here they were in a supposedly peaceful mountain village far removed from the crimes of the big towns and cities. Yet, in the space of only three months, a girl had gone missing in mysterious circumstances and two people had been bludgeoned to death.

The Glacier Guest House, like most other buildings in Sonamarg, was boarded up for the winter and the village had an abandoned, ghostly feel to it. A taxi arrived and deposited a young couple close to the tourist centre. They were Hindus and Reta wondered if they had been recently married. The girl was wearing a silk *saree* which seemed totally impractical; not only would it get splattered by mud from the street, it also provided little protection against the biting cold.

They had come from the direction of Srinagar, suggesting that their taxi driver either didn't mind taking risks or had been offered a bigger tip. Kenny, who by this time was getting to know something of the Kashmiri character, put it down to the latter.

The MacDonalds took a last look at the village and began the journey along the ice-encrusted road to where they hoped their taxi would be waiting for them. Derek was relieved to be leaving but Sam had enjoyed his brief visit to this strange place which seemed like a shanty town in the Yukon after the gold prospectors had gone. He was impressed by the staggering beauty of the mountains and he consoled himself in the knowledge that even had he been able to paint, no one would have believed that the sky was such a deep blue.

On the way back he saw a Gujar with a pony and negotiated a price for the hire of the scrawny animal. He and Derek took turns at riding it, but the conditions underfoot made the experience even more uncomfortable than usual and both boys were glad when they saw their taxi waiting in the distance.


The trip to Sonamarg had been worth while. Kenny's and Reta's reason for going there was simply to let Sam and Derek see the village whose name had, for the past four months, figured so prominently in the lives of all the family. The press had gone for the angle of a distraught family making a Christmas pilgrimage to a place that, for them, had become a shrine. One paper even fabricated a story that the MacDonalds had taken a birthday cake with them. But for the MacDonalds the trip had a more practical purpose. They were looking out for a building which a close friend of the family, Betty Kelly, had seen in a dream. Betty Kelly, a middle-aged woman with three grown-up children, lived with her husband, Terry, in a comfortable semi-detached house in Aberdeen's Deeside Gardens. Coincidentally, the Kellys' home was only a few hundred yards from where Alison and her friend, Chrissie Kennedy, shared digs in 1979 and Alison frequently saw the couple who had been friends of her parents for many years.

Terry Kelly, a Roman Catholic, had worked alongside Kenny in H.M. Customs and Excise at Heathrow Airport, often sharing jokes and pulling one another's legs about religion. Their wives, too, found they had a lot in common and so it was a happy coincidence when both families found themselves transferred to Aberdeen at roughly the same time.

Betty Kelly, a durable Scot of staunch Presbyterian beliefs, was not the sort of person to let her emotions get the better of her. Her practical stoicism helped her through life's ups and downs and when Alison went missing she was, for Reta, a great source of support and encouragement.

Betty, a pragmatist by nature, was not given to fanciful ideas of the supernatural yet, right from the moment she heard the news, she felt sure that Alison was still alive. She could not account for it and in some ways it defied her natural instincts, yet it was a powerful sensation and it left her slightly perturbed.

One night, some three months after Alison's disappearance, she was lying in bed when a strange thing happened. It was just after midnight and she was not yet quite asleep. Suddenly she saw in her mind's eye a picture so clear and precise that it could have been a photograph. She did not recognise the place but she knew it was in some way connected with Alison. Betty, now sitting upright in bed, could recall every detail of the scene that moments before had flashed through her subconscious and she immediately got out of bed to find a piece of paper and pen.

Her hurriedly produced sketch on a piece of cardboard showed a two-storey building against a backdrop of tall mountains. The building was in a field, or meadow, to the right of a winding road and next to it was a small, oddly shaped outhouse. It was this, in particular, that she associated with Alison. The scene could have been anywhere but Betty knew it was not just anywhere: it was India and the building was on the fringe of a village.

She lay awake for most of the night and by morning she was still not sure whether to tell Reta MacDonald. She felt embarrassed that she, of all people, should have experienced something so at odds with her matter-of-fact approach to life. She wondered, also, whether she might be raising false hopes by passing on such information.

However, so strong was the association between her vision and Alison's disappearance that she felt compelled to telephone Reta to describe the scene.

Reta's reaction was that her friend's dream may, indeed, be of some value, even though it did not fit into either person's view of the order of things, and as she listened to Betty's description of the place she felt a shiver run through her body.

Now, in Kashmir, Reta carried Betty's drawing around with her wherever she went, looking all the time for a building that resembled the one depicted so vividly in her friend's dream.

Several days had elapsed since the announcement in the media of the big increase in the reward money and still no one had come forward with information. The MacDonalds had hoped that the inducement would have been enough to persuade someone to break their silence. It was no longer a question of 'if' they would be reunited with Alison but 'when' and they had real hopes that this time they would be taking their daughter home with them.

*Kenny MacDonald*

*Alison MacDonald*

*Houseboat, Dal Lake, Srinagar*
*Alison MacDonald, Liz Merry stayed here in August 1981*

*River Sindh, Sonamarg*

*Telegram from Reta MacDonald to husband
informing him about appeal fund*

*Telegram from Liz Merry about Alison's disappearance*

But there were no new leads to follow and Kenny found himself going over old ground. He was in occasional contact with Gulam Nabi and Amin Chapri but Aslem Beg, from whom suspicion had not been entirely removed, was now in hospital in Delhi being treated for his asthma.

Marharaj Machama called on the MacDonalds at the Rays' home, where they were still staying, but he was no longer directly involved in the case and could offer little in the way of hard facts. The boys liked Machama. He was good company and had an excellent command of English. He was also much taken by Sam's portable cassette recorder and returned the next night with a wad of notes with which to buy it. Sam, seeing the cash emerge from a pocket in the policeman's uniform, flexed his entrepreneurial muscles and got himself a good deal. He and his younger brother both enjoyed their visit to Kashmir. He didn't much like Kala's curries and ate, whenever possible, at some of the restaurants downtown that did Chinese and English cooking. One of the family's favourites was the not inappropriately named Alkasalsar, a popular eating place for those seeking respite from spicey Indian food.

In Ghulam Mohammed's leather shop, Kenny bought his wife an embroidered sheepskin coat like the hippies used to wear in the sixties and they each bought small gifts for relatives back home: a fur hat for Reta's father, a purse for Mairi and a canvas and leather holdall in which to carry their few souvenirs, including the two *kangris* they had purchased earlier. Most of the nuns at the Presentation Convent had gone away for the winter but the three stalwart souls who remained promised to keep a lookout for anyone resembling Alison. One said she would peer under womens' veils, discreetly, of course. On 30 December the family flew to Delhi. They were now on their way home. This time their sadness at leaving was made worse by the fact that, in spite of the reward and all the publicity, no new information had emerged about the mystery of their daughter's disappearance. They were utterly convinced she was still alive, but where was she?

As they arrived back in Edinburgh, just in time for Hogmanay, they wondered whether they would ever see Alison again. Soon it would be another year, a year they hoped would bring them the joy they longed for so much.

97

# 10

It was half past nine in the morning and someone was knocking on Kenny's door.

"There's a phone call for you Mr. MacDonald. Could you follow me please."

News of his return to Kashmir had appeared in the previous morning's edition of *Aftab* and Amin Chapri had wasted no time in contacting him.

"I phoned you many times yesterday but you were not in," said Chapri. "You have come back. That is good. I have news for you. It is very important."

Chapri did not elaborate but insisted on seeing Kenny as soon as possible. They agreed to meet that evening in Kenny's room in the manse.

It was 11 February 1982 and he had been back in Srinagar for three days. Six weeks had gone by since he and Reta had returned to Edinburgh but this time he was alone, more determined than ever to find his daughter.

The Rays were still away but, in any case, he had decided against staying with them. The school had become a very conspicuous place and anyone with information about Alison might be deterred from calling there for fear of being seen. So he went to the Church of North India where he knew accommodation was sometimes available at low rent in the manse, and asked if he could be put up.

The room was bare except for a simple bed and a chair. The temperature could not have been more than a degree or two higher than outside where winter maintained its icy grip, but a house-boy brought a small electric fire to take the edge off the chill. There was also a simple electric stove on which he could cook simple meals. On the evening of 11 February Kenny looked out of a window of the two-storey building and saw a strange figure emerge from the dark. Whoever it was had decked himself out in the most eye-catching disguise he had ever seen. The stranger was wearing a white-belted coat, green trousers tucked into knee-length brown leather boots and around his neck was a tartan scarf. His head was covered by a black leather balaclava and dark eyes peered through a pair of snow goggles.

Amin Chapri rang the bell and climbed upstairs to Kenny's room. They shook hands and the visitor took off his coat and pushed his goggles to his forehead. He looked fit and had grown a beard since Kenny had last seen him.

Chapri said that he had read in *Aftab* that Kenny was back and questioned whether the publicity was wise. What he had to say was long-winded and garbled but, unlike the last time the two men met, he claimed to know a great deal about what had happened to Alison and where she was now.

Kenny was highly sceptical about anything this man said, but he listened, anyway, as Chapri poured out his story. He said that he and his two colleagues, Nabi and Yagub, had been working on the case non-stop and were now 'only one wall away from Alison'. She was being held in a 'rich' house only 10 kilometres from here; of this he was certain. Two months earlier she had been unwell, perhaps from the mental pressures on her, but she had now fully recovered. The motive of the kidnappers was marriage.

Kenny paled at the idea of his daughter being sold as a wife to some wealthy Indian. He was aware of the trade in brides in this part of the world and it had occurred to him many times before that Alison might by now have been forcibly married off to look after, or even to bear, someone's child, but this was the first time that anyone had claimed to have evidence to support the theory. Chapri said the kidnappers operated as a gang and any attempt to free Alison would be highly dangerous. If he tried to get her out both he and the girl might be killed and he wanted to know if Kenny had access to guns. He would also need air tickets and cash for himself and his two colleagues because afterwards they would not be safe.

Chapri said the double murder in Sonamarg had worked in their favour because the police, who were still engaged in the inquiry, would not have the resources to start interfering in his efforts to rescue Alison. If the exercise was to succeed it was vital that the police were not involved. He said he would need a message from Kenny to his daughter telling her to trust whoever went to get her. She would then be taken to a 'safe house' in Srinagar, possibly a houseboat where she could be reunited with her father. He said that immediate delivery of the reward money was not important, he could collect the cash later. He would return at six o'clock the following evening to explain what had to be done next.

He departed as stealthily as he had arrived, leaving Kenny to ponder the extraordinary hypothesis that had just been laid before him. His first instinct was to regard the whole thing as a pack of lies but he could not afford to close his mind to anything, no matter how unreliable the source, and that night he lay awake wondering if he really was about to see his precious daughter again. In his diary he wrote:

1. He knows where Alison is.

2. He knows who the kidnapper is.

3. 'They' have decided to get rid of her because of her unco-operativeness and the continued publicity.

4. They want a good deal; money and trouble for someone else.

5. My hunch says it is still political.

After he returned to Srinagar three days earlier Kenny had discovered that there had been several other developments. Javed Machdoomi, had been on a traffic course in Delhi but he had briefly interviewed H. K. Singh before passing him over to a colleague. As it turned out the police were satisfied that the Sikh, an employee in the Indian Army's Military Engineering Services, was not implicated in any way.

But there was another line of inquiry to follow. A conversation had been overheard at the Srinagar Golf Club between a bank manager and an insurance agent. The insurance man had apparently been in Sonamarg on, or near, 16 August, when he saw two white girls talking to a Turk in the tourist restaurant. The Turk seemed to be rather interested in the two pretty girls.

There was no way of knowing, of course, if the girls were Alison and Liz but every scrap of information, no matter how innocuous, had to be checked. Kenny then began trying to trace the insurance man.

On his second day back he had planned to go to Kangan where Nazir, the houseboy at the Glacier Guest House, was working during the winter. He had no particular reason for interviewing him again, other than getting him to repeat the story he had given many times before. However it was snowing heavily that morning and he decided that Kangan, about half way between Srinagar and Sonamarg, might be cut off. Instead he spent the day reading and in the evening went to the Alkasalsa for a meal. That day, Alison's photograph appeared in one of the local papers. It was a previously unpublished picture of his daughter that he had given to the local press two days earlier. That night, as he wrote to Reta at home in Edinburgh, he felt curiously content.

Amin Chapri turned up for their meeting a quarter of an hour early. From the window of his room Kenny could see him walking through the slush towards the manse and as the visitor approached Kenny prayed fervently that the news would be encouraging.

"You are a very lucky man," said Chapri. "Everything will be all right but it will take time."

Kenny fought to contain his anger. He had allowed himself to think this meeting would lead him to Alison but, not for the first time, the slippery figure sitting opposite, seemed to be talking gibberish.

The substance of the conversation, recorded in Kenny's diary, was this: Alison had been seen alive and well; she now had short hair. She had been kidnapped, possibly to be used as a political hostage in the run-up to the forthcoming state elections. It could take four months to secure her release; on the other hand she could be free in a fortnight. "Be patient. Be a good father," said Chapri. "The reward money isn't everything. I will collect it when this is all finished."

Later, as he sat alone in his room, Kenny tried to unfathom Chapri's confused story. He had always considered himself to be a good judge of character but he did not know what to make of the man on whose word he now attached so much importance. Only a day before he had been told Alison had been kidnapped for reasons of marriage; now he was being asked to believe that the motive was political. Was this wily character's latest theory the product of a sick mind or did he really know something? Kenny's total inability to form an opinion on this question was reflected in the notes he entered in his diary that evening.

1. Alison has been seen alive and well by someone.

2. Short haircut.

3. Kidnapper probably connected to political family.

4. Election in 4/5 months

5. Three musketeers know who has Alison, where she is etc. But they are playing another hand altogether. Blackmail? Discredit family before election?

6. They are to discuss this weekend what to do. I pushed my impatience and pointed out that six months ago Ghulam Nabi said 'maybe six months' so after another four months, what then?

John and Catherine Ray had by now returned from their annual holiday and that evening, over supper, Kenny told them about his latest meeting with Chapri. As he walked back to the manse just before midnight he was still no nearer knowing whether he had got caught up in an elaborate web of double-dealing and deceipt.

In the morning the pastor brought Kenny his breakfast as he had done every day for almost a week. In the cold stone-floored room he appreciated the hot tea and distinctively flavoured Kashmiri bread, still slightly warm from the oven.

Chapri phoned shortly afterwards. He said it was vital that he dealt only with Kenny. He did not want the police, the army or any other officials involved, not even John Ray. He would tell him everything he knew the following evening. But it was not safe for him to come to the manse; they should meet at the shikari stand opposite Nehru Park. Then he hung up.

In his diary Kenny wrote:

1. He's scared to let too much out in case I cause trouble. ie, three of them plus political kidnapper.

2. He does not want me to do anything just now as he does not know how near to breaking point I might be.

3. This week-end should decide what is going to happen.

It was still only mid-morning and he decided to go to Kangan to see Nazir, the houseboy at the Glacier Guest House. Nazir, a tall, quiet lad of about eighteen had been on duty on the day of Alison's disappearance and Kenny wanted to be certain that his information about his daughter's movements that morning was correct.

Kenny found Nazir without any difficulty and asked him to repeat what he had told both him and the police some months earlier. Alison, said the houseboy, was the first of the guests to get up. For breakfast she had omelette and toast. The time was about eight o'clock. When the Italians and Aslem Beg appeared, some time later, she joined them for a cup of tea. Nazir said he did not see Alison leave because, after ten, he was busy serving tea to the day trippers arriving by bus from Srinagar. Later that day he noticed she had not returned but thought nothing of it  People returning from the pilgrimage to the Amarnath Cave a week earlier were still turning up in the village and it was not uncommon for western tourists to talk to the pilgrims about this important Hindu event. Some foreigners even stayed with them for a day or two.

Kenny then changed tack. He had received an unsigned note from someone in Sonamarg, possibly a shopkeeper, alleging that the guest house owner and the tourist officer had gone on a heavy drinking spree on the night of 16 August. This had no apparent bearing on Alison's disappearance except for two things: why should the owner have denied it, and why should anyone want to tell him about it?

"Is the owner a heavy drinker?" asked Kenny.

"No,"said Nazir. "He used to drink a lot but not now."

"And the tourist officer?"

"I do not know the tourist officers. I never go to that part of the village."

That evening Kenny received a phone call at the Rays' home. It was the Army and the person at the other end wanted to know if he could call round. Twenty minutes later, a jeep pulled up and a man in uniform jumped out. He introduced himself as an officer in the intelligence section and explained that he had an interest in the case. He had friends who were involved in mysticism and if Kenny cared to tell them everything about his daughter's disappearance he might be able to help.

Kenny's suspicions were immediately aroused. The officer, a Jain with the rank of colonel, must surely have had access to army records on the case, so why did he want to go over ground that was already well documented?

Kenny wondered if the colonel's story was simply a cover for finding out if he suspected a military connection in his daughter's disappearance. There was no shortage of Kashmiris eager to place the blame on troops whom they regarded as an army of occupation and there were also Kenny's frequent meetings with Amin Chapri, a man who had never concealed his contempt for the Indian Army. Was this officer, who claimed his mission was personal, really trying to establish whether Kenny had become embroiled, albeit innocently, in the Kashmiri Liberation Front? He decided that it would be unwise to say too much and told the officer only what he probably already knew.

> I have considered all manner of things but I think I'll just go along with Amin to see what happens and look to God for words of guidance.

Kenny hailed a rickshaw and set out for his 5.30 p.m. rendezvous with Amin Chapri. As the three-wheeler trundled along the bumpy road of the Boulevard, he realised he was twenty minutes too early and asked the driver to stop a good half mile short of his destination. As he walked along the walled footpath which skirted this section of the Dal Lake he could see the familiar figure of Chapri in the distance. Chapri pretended not to recognise him. Instead he kept his head slightly bowed and said quietly: 'shikari Pigeon – get in'. Kenny continued walking and among the small flotilla of shikaris moored to a concrete landing ghat he spotted the name *Pigeon* painted on a board nailed to its gaudy canopy. He got in and waited and a few minutes later Chapri joined him. Wasting no time, he cast off and began paddling towards the houseboat *Haifa*. Amin Chapri lived on the *Haifa* with his brothers and his father, a venerable figure among Srinagar's Muslims. When visitors were present women were seldom, if ever, in evidence.

They crossed the still black water of the lake and found the *Haifa* in the labyrinth of waterways that separate the islands and floating gardens. Only a few feet divided the neat row of square prowed houseboats, many with small gardens, that lined either side of the wide channel. The two men climbed the short flight of steps that descended almost to water level and entered the dimly lit reception room of one of the lake's finer houseboats. There was something very English about the room. The writing desk and lamp stands were of mahogany and the sofa and arm chairs seemed solid and well made. A huge, richly patterned rug of Kashmiri wool covered the timber floor and on the walls were paintings that might have been picked up cheap at a saleroom in Tunbridge Wells.

Once inside Chapri lit the *bokhari* (stove) and made tea. Then he sat down and spelled out his terms. He said he wanted a private business arrangement with Kenny to cover the following: a letter to Alison from her father; the reward money clarified; a guarantee that Kenny would lie low for three weeks and, finally, payment for 'his representatives'. All four conditions had to be agreed in writing.

Kenny, feeling that he had no alternative but to accept the terms, asked Chapri for a sheet of paper and began writing:

Dearest Alsoon. Please co-operate with this man for escape only. Keep your chin up. 'He that is with us.'

Dad XX

'Alsoon' was Kenny's pet name for his daughter. He was the only person who called her that and he knew that if he wrote 'Alsoon' she would be in no doubt about the authenticity of the letter. Chapri took the piece of paper, folded it up into a small square and concealed it in chewing gum paper. The rest of the agreement was completed in duplicate with each party retaining a signed copy. Chapri produced a small mountain of documents on the case – newspaper cuttings, maps, photographs and notes – and Kenny knew instantly that the man with whom he had entered into a formal agreement, was deadly serious.

Having got what he wanted Chapri delivered his latest account about what had happened to Alison. But this time, he told Kenny, it was not conjecture, it was fact. His information had come from his 'representatives' and he was convinced of its accuracy.

He said Alison had been abducted by an Army officer and was now being held near Srinagar. Three months earlier, in November, she had had a miscarriage and was taken in a white military ambulance to a civilian hospital. But within an hour of arriving there she was transferred to an Army hospital where she was kept in a private ward reserved for officers. She remained at the hospital for three days before being taken back to a military camp where a nurse visited her daily. Chapri said his information came from two nurses, both Kashmiri, who worked at the Army hospital, one on day shift, the other on nights. A week ago one of the nurses was herself taken to hospital having been badly beaten up. Chapri wrote down the nurses' names and handed the piece of paper to Kenny but warned him not to attempt to contact them unless he, Chapri, disappeared.

He said he knew in which area Alison was being held but would not know until later, perhaps the following day, perhaps not for three weeks, the exact location of the house.

"You must do nothing for three weeks," he said. "No one can help you except myself and my helpers. If the kidnappers find out that we know who they are, they will move your daughter and then we will never find her."

Kenny had listened to Chapri's declamation with growing incredulity. Even if his daughter had become pregnant through rape – by any other means was unthinkable – surely the military would not be so idiotic as to take her to a civilian hospital where the crime might be exposed. And, given the publicity surrounding her disappearance, wouldn't someone, other than the two nurses, have sensed that something was going on, something that amounted to an Army cover-up?

Kenny desperately did not want to believe what he had just been told. But he had learned to approach every possibility with an open mind and Chapri had, for once, been quite specific in his allegations. It was not beyond the bounds of possibility that he was telling the truth.

Now, having agreed to Chapri's conditions, there was little Kenny could do for three weeks other than hope and pray.

For Kenny MacDonald this was perhaps the most difficult time of all. Ever since he first set foot in India he had hardly stopped searching for Alison. He had badgered and bullied, coaxed and cajoled. And on a people not unknown for their vanity he had used his most potent weapon of all – flattery. Now, six months to the day since his daughter disappeared, he was a consenting partner to an agreement that rendered him powerless. All he could do was wait.

The previous day he went to see the two policemen who had been most closely involved in the case. He wanted to know what they really thought had happened to his daughter, not what they said publicly or what they thought he wanted to hear.

"She's dead," said Superintendent Javed Machdoomi. "She either died in the river or some soldiers got her."

He directed the same question to Inspector Maharaj Machama. "She's dead but I don't know how. I'm puzzled."

That night he reflected on what they had said and refused to accept what a growing number of people now believed.

I assume, then, she's alive and that God says so. Three and a half million Kashmiris working for me: Lord, Lord, if we could but teach them about Jesus.

In the days that followed he kept out of the limelight. A request by All-India Radio for an interview was refused and he shunned all press publicity.

It snowed for much of the time and the simple room in which he was cooped up every night took on a more desolate appearance. He kept loneliness at bay by visiting the many friends he had made. The Rays, as always, were a great source of strength and encouragement and he often went to their home for his evening meal. He had been befriended by Shahid Ali Khan, a shopkeeper he referred to as 'the brass man'. Khan was not involved in the investigation in any way and Kenny welcomed his company on the few occasions on which he was able to relax, often over a glass of tea. Once, when he offered to pay, 'the brass man' insisted: "You are a guest in our country so I hope you will accept our hospitalisation". Kenny smiled broadly and pointed out that what he hoped his friend meant was 'hospitality'.

Once Inspector Machama invited him to his home for a meal. When he arrived at the policeman's modest house he received a typically effusive Indian welcome. But when the food was about to be served he was more than a little perplexed to discover that he was required to eat alone in a room separate from the family. On inquiring why, he was told that, as devout Hindus, the family could not share their table with someone who, under Hindu laws, was deemed to be 'unclean'. He accepted the explanation with equanimity and at the end of an otherwise enjoyable stay, went into the kitchen to compliment Mrs Machama and the other women of the household on their culinary skills. Only later, when he related the experience to John Ray, a seasoned observer of Kashmiri customs, did he learn that his presence in a non-Hindu kitchen would have been anathema to the Machama family and they would have been compelled to scrub it from top to bottom after his departure.

The short days of winter were long in passing as Kenny waited for word from Chapri. For much of the time he was alone with his thoughts.

> Lord, what encouragement to Thy praying people if Alison is restored alive. What a thought for those who don't believe. Lord, Lord, be with Alison.

On 1 March he moved in with the Rays. His self-imposed exile in the manse had lasted four weeks but now, with nothing very much happening, he felt there would be no harm in staying with his friends again. His bill for the spartan accommodation was not much but when he attempted to settle the outstanding amount, the pastor declined to accept any money, saying that Kenny was a guest of the Church of North India.

Although he was obliged, under his agreement with Chapri, to keep a low profile, he had continued his investigation of the insurance agent who had apparently seen a Turk talking to two girls in a restaurant in Sonamarg at about the time Alison and Liz were in the village. The story sounded odd. What was a Turk doing there? And why should the insurance man mention it in conversation at the Srinagar Golf Club?

Whenever Kenny attempted to contact the insurance man he never seemed to be in his office. Eventually he concluded that the man was, for some reason, trying to avoid him. On one occasion a clerk told him to return in the afternoon but when he did so he was again told the man he wanted to see was not there. "Tell him that if he won't see me, he'll jolly well see the police," barked Kenny. But, this time, instead of giving up he came back five minutes later to find that the insurance man had been there all along.

As he questioned him the reasons for his bashfulness became clear. The man had been leering at the two pretty girls in shorts and was ashamed of being found out. It was no more sinister than that. Besides, he could prove that the incident happened on 19 August, so the two girls could not have been Alison MacDonald and Liz Merry. Kenny was satisfied with the man's explanation and left.

During this period he kept out of the way of the authorities, relying, instead, for information on the many people – ordinary Kashmiris he had got to know and whose help and support he valued. Much of the news they provided was hearsay and probably not accurate but overall it contributed to his understanding of Kashmir and its people. Rumours about what had happened to Alison abounded, with most people believing, or wanting to believe, that the military was responsible. But while this was always a possibility, it was not, in his view, the most likely explanation. As far as he was concerned the person who seemed to hold the key to the mystery was Amin Chapri.

Eighteen days after their meeting on the *Haifa*, Chapri phoned Kenny to give him further instructions. They were to meet at 2 p.m. at a bridge at Dal Gate. Kenny's heart was pounding as he prepared to leave. Catherine Ray was very excited and they all prayed that this would be the breakthrough they had waited for so long. As he walked the one and a half miles from the Mission School to the Dal Gate, Kenny was trembling and his stomach was in a knot. He felt that it was now only a matter of time before he was reunited with his daughter. The two men met, as arranged, and agreed to go somewhere quiet to talk. On the way there Chapri said there was nothing new to report but considering their agreement ended in only three days time, Kenny thought the Kashmiri seemed strangely confident, even bullish.

They came to an alley from which a flight of stairs led them to a bar. Chapri ordered a brandy but Kenny didn't like the look of the bottle and, suspecting that its contents might be adulterated, chose not to have anything. Very little emerged from the conversation and that night Kenny wrote in his diary:

> Long chat about nothing. Is he concealing something? Lord, thou knowest. He wants me to have dinner with him in his houseboat, *Haifa*, at about 7 p.m. tomorrow, the 5th. Meet him at Hotel Mazda at 1830. I am not dejected but very puzzled. Could he be having me on? Lord, Lord when is thy time?

The following day Kenny met Chapri as arranged and the two men took a shikari to the *Haifa*. Chapri lit the boukari and launched into his latest theory. He again alleged that Alison had been abducted by an army officer and was now married to him. The officer, he said, had since been transferred to the town of Udhampur, about 160 miles south of Srinagar on the way to Jammu. Chapri claimed his information had come from an Army 'mole', a major, who was travelling to Udhampur the following day with the note Kenny had written almost three weeks earlier. The major would get Alison to write something on the back of the note and, all being well, he would be back in Srinagar on 8 March. Chapri also told Kenny that he had established that his daughter was being detained in one of two houses at a military base in Udhampur.

> He is so plausible. Is he telling the truth? Smokescreen? He *does* know where Alison is, which is the main thing.

## 11

Forty miles to the south of Srinagar is the small town of Anantnag. Here the road forks, one route turning north-east to the beautiful valley in which the village of Pahalgam is situated, the other continuing south to Udhampur and Jammu. Anantnag is known for the curative properties of its sulphur springs, the largest of which is said to be the home of Ananta, the serpent on which Vishnu reclines and from where the town takes its name, 'Abode of Ananta'. The place is of some significance to Hindus and every October on the fourteenth day of a full moon fortnight there is a festival in which people fast and pour rice and milk into the spring to feed the goldfish.

But Anantnag also has a small population of Christians and it was here that Kenny MacDonald arrived on Sunday 7 March to preach to a congregation of about 100 in the chapel of the local hospital. Everyone knew about the bearded Scottish minister but very few people in this pleasant little town understood English so his sermon, on Ruth, was translated as he spoke. it was an unusual experience but it seemed to work. Later, by the river, he watched kingfishers flit from rock to rock and as he returned to Srinagar, now emerging from the smoky days of winter, he felt refreshed.

Chapri phoned the next day to say he had nothing new to report but Kenny was not satisfied with this and insisted on seeing him. Forty minutes later they met outside the Mazda restaurant. Chapri said the major, whom he claimed was working for him, had now returned from Udhampur. He, personally, had not yet spoken to him but he had learned, through an intermediary, that Kenny's note to Alison had been returned with two numbers on it. These, said Chapri, were the numbers of officers' quarters at Udhampur. Alison had been forced into marriage and was being detained in one or the other of them. Chapri also claimed that the officer responsible for the kidnapping was the son of a top-ranking soldier, now retired.*

* Chapri gave the retired officer's rank, making identification of the son easy.

111

Kenny was still unable to decide whether he was being fed the devilish outpourings of a twisted mind. Had he become a tap to be turned on and off whenever Chapri wanted to give vent to his obsessive hatred of the Army? Or did the man really have, or believe he had, information about Alison? Kenny told him he wanted to talk to the 'tame' major for himself. If the officer wouldn't talk to him, then perhaps he would talk to the military police. Chapri nodded and told Kenny he would phone him the following afternoon.

That evening Kenny returned to the Mission School to discover that earlier two Army officers had called. They departed without leaving a message or saying who they were.

One.month to the day since his return to Kashmir, Kenny MacDonald was given the name of the man to whom his daughter was allegedly married. But he was in a quandary about how much significance to attach to the word of Amin Chapri, a man whose story seemed to change each time he saw him. Chapri claimed to have established a connection between the Signals' base at Sonamarg and the Army camp at Udhampur. He then told him precisely what his sources had said. (Amin Chapri's allegations, recorded in detail in Kenny MacDonald's diary, were never substantiated and are thus only hearsay.)

By now more sceptical than ever about Chapri's pronouncements, Kenny said that he would check the information personally.

That evening he told John Ray what he had learned and together they considered ways in which Chapri's extraordinary claims might be investigated. The headmaster suggested they should seek the help of two Christian Brothers who often called at the school. They had good contacts in the Army and might be able to provide an introduction to senior military personnel in Jammu. He also knew of a Christian major in the Army who might be able to help.

That night Kenny wrote in his diary: 'I feel sad that we are not as close as we thought.'

The next day he began trying to corroborate what Chapri had told him. The inquiry now centred on the Signals' base at Sonamarg but Sonamarg was still cut off by deep snow and he had to confine his inquiries to Srinagar. Neither Machama or Machdoomi were in when he phoned but he was able to find the tourist officer resident there the previous summer. He confirmed what Kenny already knew: that nine or ten soldiers were stationed at the camp at the time of Alison's disappearance and that there was another Signals base at Baltal, ten miles from Sonamarg.

It was not long, however, before inconsistencies began to emerge in Chapri's story. Chapri had said that the Army camp, at Udhampur, in which Alison was being held was called Sadwari. In fact, Sadwari was in Jammu, a city forty miles to the south. Later when challenged about the error Chapri agreed he had made a mistake.

The following Monday Kenny decided to go to Jammu to establish whether there was any substance in Chapri's allegations. A friend of the Rays provided him with an introduction to a high-ranking officer in the armed forces who might be able to help. Normally Kenny would have gone by bus but part of the road had been washed away by landslides. Fortunately, depending on the determination of their drivers, taxis were able to circumnavigate the mud and rocks and Kenny found himself in Jammu after a three-and-a-half-hour journey. Getting there had been no small miracle because at one point, when he had had nothing better to do, he counted no less than 243 vehicles, including a convoy of army lorries, stuck in a traffic jam!

In Jammu, a city of some 200,000 people, he made for the home of Bishop Aziz Williams who had once addressed the General Assembly of the Church of Scotland in Edinburgh. The bishop welcomed him and, after hearing what he had to say, suggested that he speak to two Christian acquaintances, both officers in the Indian Army. But when the officers, a major and a captain, arrived at the bishop's house that afternoon it became clear that, although sympathetic, they were too scared to get involved. Kenny realised that he would therefore have to find other ways of getting into the camp at Sadwari.

Fortunately the Rays' friend was more helpful. The man, a Christian, said he would do all he could but pointed out that he would be risking his career if he were found out. However the officer, who adopted the pseudonym 'Moses', said he was willing to take a risk given the gravity of the allegations. The following morning he and Kenny drove through the camp gates as though they were visiting dignitaries. Soldiers stopped to salute and 'Moses', resplendent in full uniform, went briskly about his business.

The bluff had worked. Kenny was able to check, almost unhindered, the information provided by Amin Chapri. But his doubts about its accuracy were reflected in his diary entry that night. 'Yes, partly true, but essentials not.'

He was able to confirm that the officers' quarters, the numbers of which were written on the back of his note to Alison did, in fact, exist. But no one of the name* he had been given, lived there. Nevertheless it was possible that the officer had been posted elsewhere and 'Moses' agreed to make further inquiries and to contact Kenny in Srinagar.

> Went to see Ali. Laid it on the line re duff gen.

By now Kenny could scarcely contain his anger every time he thought about Chapri. But his feelings were directed mainly at himself for still not being able to make up his mind about whether or not he was being duped. On his return from Jammu he learned that another link in the chain had proved fallacious and when he met Chapri he told him that he was highly sceptical of the Kashmiri's claims. He stopped short of calling him a liar, but by now he distrusted him deeply and started referring to him in his diary as 'Ali' after Ali Baba.

But there was one piece of good news. Word had reached Mary McLaren in Delhi, by way of Norman McArthur's† telex machine that Kenny and Reta's other daughter, Mairi, had just given birth to her second child, a boy. The telex said that it was a toss-up between naming him James William or Jock Wallace but the joke had to be explained to John and Catherine Ray who knew little about Scottish football personalities. (Jock Wallace was formerly the manager of Rangers Football Club.)

Meanwhile Kenny kept asking questions everywhere he went. The police file on Alison MacDonald remained open but their

---

*Kenny knew the name. It also emerged there were only six people of this name in the Indian Army.

†Norman McArthur, a friend of the MacDonalds in Stornoway, had a telex machine by which information was sometimes sent to Kenny in Srinagar.

day-to-day involvement in the case had now ceased. One of the few scraps of information that came his way concerned Ibrahim Chapri, brother of Amin. He had been to see the Christian missionaries, the same missionaries who had spotted his name in a guest house register at Narannag the previous summer. He told them that some months previously he had provided a European girl with free accommodation and meals. When the girl, who said she had no money, asked for a bigger room, Ibrahim told her to contact his uncle. He did not know her name or where she was now.

It was clear from his description, and the dates, that the girl was not Alison but Kenny was nevertheless puzzled. Who was the girl and why had Ibrahim told the missionaries about her, when he knew they would pass the information on to him? Was it, he wondered, a sign that there was more Ibrahim wanted to tell him?

A few days later Kenny was walking past the bus station in Srinagar when a group of taxi drivers ran towards him. "Come quick, come quick," they shouted. He asked what was going on and was told that a white girl had moments earlier asked them for directions to the mission school. They wondered whether the girl was Alison.

Seconds later Kenny saw the girl in the distance. She was carrying a suitcase and from the back she looked just like his daughter. She had the same colour of hair and was of similar height. She was even wearing the same kind of clothes. Kenny ran after her, his heart thumping with excitement. As he caught up with her the girl turned round. It was not his daughter and his hopes which had been so fleetingly raised sank once again, only this time deeper.

A few days later he was home in Edinburgh not knowing whether he would ever return to India.

# 12

Amin Chapri shook my hand and invited me to sit down. There was a quiet elegance about the room in which we sat and the furnishings were tasteful and discreet. The suite had probably been recovered more than once and the fabrics were a little worn in places but the seats had a slightly crumpled well-used look of quality about them and it occurred to me we might easily have been in the drawing room of a smart country house. Instead we were on the houseboat *Haifa* on the Dal Lake, the same vessel on which, more than three years earlier, Kenny MacDonald had heard Amin Chapri spill out his various theories about Alison's disappearance.

I had gone to the *Haifa* to ask Amin Chapri what he knew about Alison's disappearance. Not unnaturally, he seemed suspicious of my motives and it was not until our second meeting, the following evening, that he talked more freely. His English was stilted and he frequently repeated himself but the substance of what he had to say was this:

I became involved in the case partly because of the reward money. But it was not only that: I am a mountain guide and searching for someone missing in the mountains was a good job for me. Also, it was the effect of Mr MacDonald on my conscience. I think the girl, Alison, was taken away by someone. But it was not the mountain or village people. They are afraid of the police and would not do this thing. I believe it was the Army who did it. The area is always busy with soldiers. She was a very innocent girl and I think she was watched for some time before. Then she was invited by the Army people and after that anything could happen. I am sure it was not civilians who did this. I cannot say how long she was alive afterwards: I think it was perhaps six or seven months. Maybe she is still alive, I am not sure. The information we got was that she was in a hospital in Srinagar about three months later. I think I am 90% sure this information is correct because there were other things. There were two nurses on duty at that time: one nurse was transferred the next day to an unknown place. The other nurse is still working there. I sent someone to see her. She was very angry but she didn't talk anything about it. I think the Army made a cover-up. The police tried to find out but they are

116

very limited. They tried up to their level but they cannot go deep in these cases.

I put it to Chapri that he blamed the Army because he had been imprisoned for his activities in the Kashmiri Liberation Front. He replied:

"It's not like that. We do have our problem here. But when there is something wrong we cannot go to an officer or high authority to ask them to inquire – we are not allowed."

Again I asked him whether he fabricated a story in order to discredit the Army.

"What I say is true. I am no longer with the Kashmiri Liberation Front but I say this: I think the Army took Alison MacDonald. Everything I told her father is true."

I wondered, when I got off the tourist bus in Sonamarg's solitary street, whether the villagers would remember the name of the girl who disappeared there four years earlier. But the events of autumn 1981 – the search parties, the police and the publicity – had left a dark cloud hanging over the place and it seemed no one had forgotten Alison MacDonald. In a shop selling silk and cotton shawls I spoke to the man who appeared to be in charge. He was about 26 and had helped search for her. This is what he said:

The police came and asked the shopkeepers to join the search. But we did not go with the police. We went with the girl's father. I think about 20-25 shopkeepers took part and nearly all the shops closed down. We searched in the river, we went high in the mountains and we went all around the area of Sonamarg. But we found nothing. Everyone here thinks the Army take the girl. The soldiers, maybe just two or three, take her. They are hungry for a European girl. They make sex and then they burn her body. This is what we believe. If the Indian Army is not responsible then where is the girl? We search all the hills and the river. If she had fallen we would find her body. But we found no body, not even a hankie.

We were joined by another, older, man. Like the first he was prepared to talk on condition that he wasn't identified. He said:

The girl's father came and asked us to help him. About fifty of us took part, maybe more. We started here early in the morning and we went to the forests, but we found no clues. The European people are very frank, they talk with anybody. Maybe she talked with the military. There are many soldiers here. We suspect the military but we are not sure; we think so. The police did not arrive for three or four weeks. It was too late to find clues. The police didn't search the Army camp. They don't have permission to go into the military area, they need a special pass for that. The people here do not like the military. They only protect the border areas. Kashmiri people do not feel safe here with the military people. We can't say anything. If they come to our shops we can't say 'don't enter'. Everyone is very much afraid of the Army. They have taken other girls before – local Kashmiri girls.

Mr G. M. Sofie, editor and proprietor of the *Srinagar Times* reached for another cake and with his free hand took a futile swipe at the flies.

"One possibility is that she was kidnapped and killed," he said.

We were sitting in the garden of his home in a busy suburb off the Boulevard. A houseboy brought more tea and another plate of cakes and a small girl, whom I took to be his daughter, played nearby.

"By whom?" I asked.

"It could have been civilian people as well as armed personnel. If it had been the Army, that does not mean the whole Army. One man, or a group of men, could have done it. But I cannot say this categorically. It is only a possibility."

"Is this the most likely explanation?"

"It is not the strongest possibility, it is one of many possibilities. She could have been kidnapped by civilians. That is also possible."

"If it had been the Army, would the senior officers have known about it?"

"The officers may not necessarily have known what their subordinates do."

"In your view how many people were involved? A dozen, perhaps?"

"Not a dozen. It could be the work of just two or three soldiers or civilians. But it was not the act of one individual because she would have resisted. My 'opinion' is that she has been done away with by more than one person, but not more than five or six."

"You don't accept there was a cover-up?"

"By the military? No, I don't believe that. But I think it was the inefficiency of the police that led to her not being found."

"But wasn't the job of the police made more difficult by the Army's lack of co-operation? They weren't even allowed into the camp at Sonamarg."

"I don't know about this. But it is the ultimate job of the police to look into the matter. It is their job to investigate even the Army people."

"Why do you criticise the police?"

"We have got many crimes here, especially murders. In many cases the killers are not being caught. Sometimes the police know who the culprits are but they are still not being apprehended."

"Would you say the police are corrupt?"

"It is a criminal type of corruption in the police."

"Do you think they know more about the case than they care to admit?"

"It is not impossible that the police may have known what happened to her because anything can be expected of corrupt people."

"Is it possible they kept quiet to prevent embarrassment to the Indian Army?"

"I know nothing about that."

"Do you think she may still be alive?"

"Sometimes miracles happen but so far as the girl MacDonald is concerned I think most probably she has been killed."

"You have to remember that she was in an area infested by wild animals," said Mr J. N. Sathu, another journalist who had covered the story four years earlier. "Maybe she was attacked by a wild bear and her dead body eaten up by jackals or other wild beasts."

"The second possibility is that she was kidnapped, raped and then killed to eliminate evidence of the crime." As we sat in his flat off Residency Road I asked him who might have done that.

"Maybe it was someone in the vicinity or in Sonamarg itself. A civilian, perhaps, or, as some people in Sonamarg told me, soldiers. The third possibility is that she might have been kidnapped by civilians and then taken across the border into Pakistan-occupied Kashmir."

"Why should anyone do that?"

"Because if the kidnappers stayed on here there was every likelihood of their being detected, prosecuted and tried. And in order to avoid that situation the kidnappers might have thought it better to go into occupied Kashmir to avoid the possibility of their being found out."

"Is it possible she was sold into marriage, perhaps to a wealthy hillsman?"

"That possibility cannot be ruled out. But one point beyond my comprehension is that if she had been kept in some place in Kashmir or in Pakistan, itself, then during all these years she would surely have tried to make contact with the outside world and made known to others that she was being kept prisoner."

"Have you heard of other instances of young women being abducted for this purpose?"

"I have heard of other cases of girls being kidnapped and kept for months in the mountains or jungle areas. Sometimes the kidnapper ultimately marries her and keeps her. Not only that, but the kidnap victim is sometimes again sold to someone else as a means of making money. There are instances in which such things have happened."

"To white girls?"

"Not to my knowledge. They are always Indian girls."

"Do you think this is what happened in Alison's case?"

"I don't think so."

"Of the possibilities you have mentioned, which do you think is the most likely?"

"Because she has not appeared so far I think she is either dead or has been taken across the border and is being kept in some remote area from which she cannot be retrieved."

Then I asked him about the relationship between the police and the Army. Was it as bad as some people claimed?

"I believe the relationship is good. They co-operate with one another out of mutual interest. And there are instances when an Army man has committed a crime, minor or major, and the officers have informed the police who have taken whatever action they deemed necessary."

"In the Alison MacDonald case were the police able to interrogate the military personnel at Sonamarg?"

"What I was told shortly after Alison disappeared was that the police had tried to make inquiries but they were told that the Army had not seen her. I was told the Army hadn't seen any girl passing on that side."

"In their position, would you have been satisfied with that assurance?"

"I can't say. It is the job of the police to investigate. The police said they were satisfied."

# 13

Betty Kelly sat up in bed and wondered whether to wake her husband, Terry. She was bewildered yet she had this inexplicable feeling of contentment. Moments earlier she had been drifting between consciousness and sleep, having put down her book some twenty minutes before. Then, suddenly, just like the first time, a picture formed in her mind and she knew, instinctively, that it was associated with Alison. The picture lasted no more than a second, if that, yet minutes later she could still recall every single detail. It was as though it had been imprinted on her mind like a photographic image on paper.

The best part of a year had passed since Betty had had her first experience of this kind. On that occasion she saw a house and, more importantly, a smaller building nearby, which she felt certain was connected in some way with the disappearance of her friends' daughter. And during Kenny and Reta MacDonald's visits to Kashmir they had seen many places that bore an uncanny resemblance to the wild, rugged terrain Betty Kelly had sketched after her 'dream'. Her verbal description of the parched blades of coarse grass and the narrow, dusty road seemed to match the landscape of this mountainous corner of India and even the buildings looked similar to some they had seen on their travels. Yet there was nothing conclusive about Betty's 'picture' – far from it, and the MacDonalds knew that it could have been anywhere.

But this time it was different. As she sat up in bed, trembling with excitement, she saw what appeared to be three vaults cut into the side of a mountain. They may well have been natural caves but they had been rounded off by the hand of man to create alcoves rather like railway arches. The one on the left was smaller than the other two and near the entrance was a thorny bush. The tops of the arches were flat and grassy, again suggesting that these curious cavities were at least in part the work of man. Each was perhaps ten feet deep and behind them, in the distance, were high mountains.

There was nothing else in Betty Kelly's 'picture', only the three caves and the mountains behind. There were no people, no buildings, no signs of life; nothing, in fact, to enable her to identify the place. Yet she knew that somehow it was connected with Alison and she felt a sense of calm as though this were proof that the girl she had known since childhood had been here.

Betty lay awake wondering whether to tell the MacDonalds about her experience. Her dilemma was not so much that they might regard her as a crank but that she might be raising their hopes falsely. She was conscious of the fact that she might be perceived by others as some kind of a medium, rather like those oddballs who sometimes crop up in police investigations into missing persons – usually children. Seldom, if ever, did their visions lead anywhere and generally all they succeeded in doing was to cause the parents further anguish. Besides Betty Kelly didn't believe in spiritualism. True, she had had what might be described as premonitions in the past, but she rarely talked about these because she could see no place for such occurrences in her strong Christian beliefs.

By the time morning came she had made up her mind. She had already told her husband, Terry, about her 'dream' and had made a sketch of the scene using the pen and pad she kept by her bedside. Now she had to tell her friends, Reta and Kenny, about it.

It was Reta who answered the phone. The couple were at home in Edinburgh where Kenny was trying to catch up with his studies for the ministry, so disrupted by the events of the past eight months. His wife called him to the phone and he listened to what their friend, in Aberdeen, had to say.

"Are you still there?" asked Betty, puzzled at the silence.

"Yes, go on; go on," came the reply.

The hairs on the back of Kenny's neck were standing up. He had listened in a state of eager excitement to Betty's description of something he had seen several times in his search for Alison. She told him about the rounded arches, smooth inside and flat on top. He asked her how high they were but she was hopeless at gauging distance and had no idea whether her answer of 15-20 feet was accurate. She felt apologetic, even embarrassed at telling him something that may have meant nothing at all. But she had always felt that Alison was still alive and in spite of her awkwardness she felt she was doing the right thing.

Kenny coaxed her into continuing but there was nothing more to tell. She had described every last detail of the vision she had had some ten hours earlier. It had been a traumatic experience and some months later when she finally brought herself to tell a close friend she found the experience no less emotional. The whole business had been deeply disturbing. She had wanted to discuss it with her minister, but decided against it. On another occasion she came close to telling the senior partner in the doctor's practice where she worked as a receptionist.

Years later she was still at a loss to know why the 'pictures', this one and the first some months earlier, should have had such a profound effect on her. After all there had been other sad events in her life since Alison's disappearance. Both her mother and stepfather had died but even the loss of people so close and dear to her failed to affect her in the same way. She was aware, also, that her 'dreams', or whatever one calls the fleeting images of the mysterious, silent world of sleep or near sleep, may have entered her subconscious through innocent conversations with the MacDonalds. But she had never discussed with them the details of their search, nor had she seen photographs of the area. In fact, for someone who, apart from a holiday in Ireland, had never been abroad, there seemed no conceivable way in which she could have known anything about the geographical features of Kashmir.

Yet her visions were so clear and so lasting and so strong were the associations with Alison's disappearance that she knew that she had experienced something more than just a dream. She felt that the visions, particularly the second one, had come in the form of a message that she was obliged to pass on to Alison's parents.

Kenny MacDonald wondered if it was a message, too, because the arches Betty Kelly had described so vividly were identical to the ammunition stores he had seen at several Army camps in the remote areas of Kashmir.

# 14

Martin Humphries and Anne Armstrong arrived at the police station at Narberth in Dyfed on the evening of 15 September 1982 and, separately, made statements about their visit to Sonamarg the previous August.

Humphries and Armstrong, whom Kenny MacDonald had referred to as 'the Welsh couple' were in the village at the same time as Alison and Liz Merry and he was anxious to have their account of their stay there verified by the police.

Tracing them had been relatively straightforward. He had obtained their names and addresses from the guest book at the tourist bungalow where they shared a room with another person, Phillip Railston from Kent. Humphries had given his parents' address in Dyfed and when Kenny contacted them they immediately informed their son by letter.

*Martin Humphries. Born: 22.9.51*

I am an artist and when in this country I reside with my parents at the above address. My girlfriend is Anne Louise Armstrong from Cardiff. On 1st November 1980, with my girlfriend (Anne Armstrong) I left England for India. We flew from Heathrow in a British Airways aeroplane and went directly to Delhi, India, arriving there at 11 a.m. that same morning. During the next few months we were to travel through India. We went to Bombay and down the coast to Kerala. On the 15th August 1981, during the early evening, we arrived in Sonamarg in the province of Kashmir. We found accommodation in a tourist bungalow which was part of an hotel in the tourist centre in Sonamarg. We stayed in the furthermost room in that corridor. During March 1981, in Chamba, my girlfriend and I met Phillip Railstone from somewhere in Kent. We were to meet about every six weeks. These meetings were not prearranged and we were also able to meet at Sonamarg. Phillip Railstone stayed in the same room as us in the tourist centre. To the best of my knowledge there were no other British persons at the centre at that time. There were about a dozen other people staying at the centre. They were from various countries. During the afternoon of 18.08.81, after Phillip Railstone had left for Srinagar, Anne and myself went to a restaurant for a meal. I do not remember the name of the restaurant* but it had a front garden and the tables were beneath a

*Almost certainly the Glacier Guest House

125

wooden verandah. Alongside the eating space were rooms – about six – that were let to tourists. At this restaurant a Kashmiri waiter said: "Have you seen a Spanish* girl? She went out for a walk yesterday and has not come back. She has left her rucksack in her room," or words to that effect. I am not sure but I believe he showed us her rucksack which was red. Anne said to the waiter: "Have you reported this to the police?" The waiter said something to the effect that he had been speaking to a tourist officer and they had reached the conclusion that they should leave the matter alone as the girl had not completed the necessary tourist forms. That is all I can remember of that incident. The following day we went to Ladakh. During the second week of October 1981 I received a letter from my father. Mentioned in this letter was the fact that a PC Eggleton had called to see him regarding the disappearance of Alison McDonald (sic) from Edinburgh. I had never heard of this girl until then and I have never met her. Since we left Sonamarg we have not met Phillip Railstone. I believe he is still in the Goa region of India. On my return to my parents' home I was contacted by Kenny McDonald regarding the disappearance of his daughter. He asked me if I had seen his daughter and I replied in the negative. Kenny McDonald posted to me photographs of his daughter, one of which had been taken in the mountains of Ladakh†. I am certain I have never met Alison McDonald. During the days we were in Sonamarg I was always accompanied by my girlfriend and with the exception of 2 hours on the morning of 17.08.81 I was always accompanied by Phillip Railstone. Phillip and myself went for a walk during that morning and because I was tired I returned to my room, leaving Phillip to continue the walk. He returned to the room some two hours later. I am certain that I have not met Alison McDonald and I first heard of her when I received a letter from my father. I did not mention what the waiter had said when I spoke to Kenny McDonald because I did not remember the incident then. I am now sending a letter to Kenny McDonald containing this information. The only other matter that I can remember was that the chaulkida (hotel manager) was not present at the centre during the night of 17th and 18th August 1981. I am certain of all these dates because I have kept a diary of my visit to India.

    M Humphries.

His girlfriend's statement was as follows:

*Anne Louise Armstrong. Born: 24.2.51*

On 1st November 1980 my boyfriend and I arrived in Delhi, India, to spend some time travelling around India. We stayed in India until 4th December 1981. On 16th August 1981 we arrived at a place called

*Waiter may have confused 'Spanish' for 'Scottish'
†A misunderstanding. Alison and Liz never reached Ladakh.

Sonamarg, Kashmir, and booked into accommodation at a Government tourist bungalow. We were accompanied by Mr Phillip Railstone from the Kent area. We met Mr Railstone in India. We stayed in Sonamarg until the morning of 19th August 1981 when we travelled to Ladakh. During the time we stayed at the tourist bungalow in Sonamarg about 12 persons also stayed there. I did not know any of these persons. During the period we stayed at Sonamarg we visited a cafe-type premises and whilst there we were asked by a waiter if we had seen a Spanish girl who had gone out for a walk the evening before* and had not returned. This is the only time we heard mention of any missing person during our stay in Sonamarg. I had never heard of a girl called McDonald until we were contacted by my boyfriend, Martin Humphries' parents. They contacted us by letter at Varanasi, Uttar Pradesh. We used to send advance addresses to Martin's parents. This would have been in early October 1981. The letter informed us that a girl called McDonald had gone missing and was believed to be in our company. This letter had been sent to us as a result of the police making enquiries on behalf of the girl's father, with Martin's parents. We replied saying that to the best of our knowledge we had not met any girl by the name of McDonald. About a week or so ago I visited Martin at his parents' home. I was shown some photographs of the girl McDonald which had been sent by her father to Martin. I did not recognise the girl as any person I met or saw in India. In one of the photographs the girl was pictured in some part of Ladakh which is a place often visited via Sonamarg. I recognised the distinctive landscape of Ladakh in the photograph.† I understand the girl is from Edinburgh. If I had met or seen a Scottish girl I would have undoubtedly spoken to her as I was born in Glasgow. During the time we stayed in the tourist bungalow as far as I can remember there were no British persons in residence apart from Martin, Mr Railstone and myself. Mr Railstone left Sonamarg the day before us and I have not seen him since. With regard to the tourist bungalow in Sonamarg I would say that there were a number of buildings under the name of the tourist bungalow. There is a complex of such buildings.

Anne Armstrong

**Five days before making his statement to the police, Martin Humphries wrote to Kenny MacDonald at his home in Edinburgh. The letter said:**

Dear Ken.

Sorry I haven't been in contact with you earlier. Anne and I have been all over the country job hunting. I'm afraid to say that we both

---

*Alison went missing after going for a walk on the morning of 17/8/81.
†The photograph was, in fact, taken in Kashmir.

agree that we haven't met or seen your daughter in the photographs. But you mentioned a restaurant in our telephone conversation which I didn't remember. Anne and I talked about this place and it seems that we did try it once. It had a verandah and a very pretty front garden. The food was expensive and we didn't eat there, but it seems there was a 'Spanish' girl staying in one of the middle rooms on the verandah who had disappeared and left her baggage the day previously. We talked to the waiter who was probably the owner. He asked us if we had seen her and said he didn't know what to do. She had apparently gone out for an early evening walk the night before and not returned. On being told that all her baggage was still in the room we suggested he should contact the police. He told us that he had already discussed the matter with the tourist officer who had told him there could be trouble with the police as she had not filled in the compulsory tourist police forms. We told the waiter (as we left) that he would have to tell the police if she didn't return. We had no reason to suspect that the girl was your daughter but it could be worth looking into. We think it was probably the 18th we had this conversation with the waiter. I feel that the tourist officer and the people in the restaurant and even the police are liable to hold back the truth on these matters, as their jobs could be forfeit. There was a religious (Hindu) festival on the 15th of August at Amarnath, a day's walk from Sonamarg. We had been there and there were other tourists there. The weather had been very wet up in the mountains. I hope this has been of some help to you, good luck.

    Martin

PS. We were in Sonamarg from the 16th to the 19th when we went on to Ladakh. We saw Phil Railstone off on a bus to Srinagar on Tuesday morning, the 18th August.

Phillip Railstone, meanwhile, had remained in India and it was some months before Kenny MacDonald was able to find out his side of the story. He had learned from Martin Humphries and Anne Armstrong that Railstone had intended going to the former Portuguese Colony of Goa, a hippies' paradise on the white sands of south-west India. Kenny wrote to him there, care of poste restante, and received this air mail reply dated 16 September 1982.

Dear Mr MacDonald.

Thank you for your letter of 1.9.82. I'm afraid that I have no information of any use to you. I must take your word for it that I went for a walk of 2½ hours on the 17th. However I remember taking only two rather easy walks from the tourist hostel. The first was behind the hostel and towards the glacier but I didn't go far up the valley;

the second (the following day) I intended to explore the valley which leads to the right of the glacier but in the end I didn't cross the river and so my second walk was almost the same as the first. I also must have walked down to the bazaar but I do not remember the bridge nor did I go over to the country on the left side of the road. We had been up to Amarnath before coming to Sonamarg. The weather was lousy and there was hardly any food. At Sonamarg I was feeling unenergetic and more interested in eating then exercising. The far side of the road from the hostel was simply too far away to attract me.

The rest of Railstone's letter stated places he hoped to visit in the months ahead. He gave two post office addresses to which letters to him could be sent. This was the last contact Kenny MacDonald had with Railstone who said he planned staying in India until February or March 1983. After that he had no idea what his address would be.

The letter received by Kenny MacDonald in January 1982 offered the strangest explanation yet to the mystery of his daughter's disappearance. It was sent to him care of Mr Javed Makhdoomi, Police Headquarters, Srinagar, and was signed by one Brian Samelovich Ashkenazi. Enclosed were three lengthy documents, photostat copies of newspaper articles, a map and a photograph.

It was the photograph that first caught Kenny's attention. The black and white print, measuring 4" × 3", showed what looked like a huge coconut and the skeletal hand of some sort of animal. The caption on the back read: 'A photograph of an adult male Yeti's scalp and hand preserved as sacred relics in the Pangboche Monastery, Tibet.' The photograph was attributed to the Mount Everest Foundation.

Ashkenazi, an Indian born in the Ukraine, believed that the mountains of northern India were inhabited by yetis and claimed to have conclusive evidence to support his theory. In his letter to Kenny he said:

I have more than forty years active practical research in Kashmir and the Himalayas generally in the habits and ethnology of the Abominable Snowman (Yeti), a mysterious and little-known giant hominid, the male of which is known to abduct young, lone girls in the Himalayas

129

(including the Sonamarg region of Kashmir) and carry them away alive and unharmed to various secret caves where they keep them alive as companions and also to improve their stock. I feel and trust your daughter is still alive and will be found alive and well by us next May (1982) when I shall be visiting Kashmir for the special purpose of assisting Mr Javed Makhdoomi and you in the search for the poor, unfortunate girl. It is needless for me to say that my heart goes out to both you and Mrs MacDonald and to your sons and other relations for this most unfortunate episode and my daily prayer to God is that we may be able to relocate her and bring her back alive and well. I would suggest that you should be in Kashmir next May (1982) which is the earliest we can hope to search for her in the region where she was last seen. I have already written to Mr Makhdoomi offering him and all concerned my fullest possible assistance and co-operation in searching for her and, God willing, restoring her alive to you and Mrs MacDonald. My prayers for your well-being and fortitude in living through this period of testing and trial with hope and optimism. A very happy New Year with prospects of relocating Alison next May and restoring you, Mrs MacDonald and her to well deserved happiness.

Kindest Regards

Yours very sincerely

Brian Samelovich Ashkenazi

One of the more gratifying features of Kenny MacDonald's search for Alison was the fact that, in spite of the widespread coverage it attracted in the Indian media, he hadn't been plagued by cranks. Everyone appeared to be genuinely sympathetic and he was relieved that the pain he felt so acutely was not made worse by letters from the lunatic fringe. His first reaction, on receiving Ashkenazi's letter, was to tear it up. But the pages of correspondence, however nonsensical, were neatly typed and the man undoubtedly had a gift for writing clearly. So he read on, turning first to an eleven-page paper claiming that Alison had been taken to an underground cave, the entrance to which was under a lake between the villages of Sonamarg and Pahalgam. The gist of his hypothesis was this:

Alison had been abducted and taken away alive by an adult, male yeti (Abominable Snowman also called Van-Manas or Jungli Adim by the local people) to an underground cave, the entrance to which was under Lake Sheeshnag. It was his opinion that she was carried into the cave through an overland entrance a short distance from the south-western flank of the lake. The entrance was then blocked by the yeti and camouflaged so that no human being or other creature, with the exception of a yeti, could enter. The lake was connected by an underground waterway to another lake and this formed part of an elaborate network of passages which enabled the amphibious yetis to move about. Alison was being held in a dry cave, accessible by an air-filled passage.

It was possible that the yeti had taken her there for breeding purposes. She would be looked after with care and affection and fed on fruit, vegetables and milk preserved underground by the ice and the meat of chicken, marmots and deer hunted by the yetis. He claimed to have personally seen a group of yetis enter Lake Sheeshnag in the summer of 1967. They neither dived nor jumped in; instead they simply walked in, presumably along an underwater shelf. Some years earlier, in 1946, he had seen a group of about 15 adult yetis sunning themselves on the shore of another lake. They, too, just walked in to the water out of sight. A horseman who was with him and who had also witnessed the incident, said that on many occasions previously the yetis had threatened to carry him underground if he persisted in trespassing on their domain.

Ashkenazi also said he had spoken to a Kashmiri woman, now living in Bombay who, as an 11-year-old, took part in the 1938 pilgrimage to the Amarnath Cave. She and others in the party saw sixty or seventy yetis disappear under the waters of Lake Sheeshnag. They waited for half an hour for them to reappear, but in vain. He said that because the lake was frozen over in winter, it would be impossible to recover Alison before the onset of summer. Then frogmen and divers should be brought into the search. He went on to say that he had evidence that a male yeti could successfully mate with a human girl and vice versa. He personally knew a 16-year-old boy in Pakistan from 1947-50 whose mother was a yeti and whose father was an army officer.

Kenny regarded Ashkenazi's rambling dissertation as utter claptrap. But the Indian press were less dismissive and Ashkenazi's extravagant claims were covered by a number of newspapers. The *Indian Express* carried a four-paragraph agency report quoting Ashkenazi as saying that the cave in which Alison was being held could be located 'only with dowsing rods – a kind of water divining rod'. But the brasher *Sunday Mid-Day* newspaper splashed the story over its front page. It quoted him as saying he had encountered a group of yetis at the Thajiwas Glacier near Sonamarg in 1967. They were 'of gigantic stature – about 12 feet in height, stark naked with lush hair, long claws, enormously long arms and comparatively short legs. Their scalps had a cone-like appearance and their ape-like faces had flaring nostrils. I had to beat a hasty retreat as they descended upon me, gesticulating wildly that I had intruded upon their territory'.

The article continued:

> Dr. Lobsang Rampa, the well-known Tibetan lama and author seems to verify Ashkenazi's belief, in his book, *The Third Eye*: 'There are tales of lonely women being carried away by male yetis. That may be one way by which yetis continue their line. Certainly some nuns have confirmed this fact to me by revealing that one of their order had been abducted by a yeti in the night.'
>
> Another interesting account of girls being kidnapped by male yetis is given by Odette Tchernine in her book *The Snowman and Company*: She (the daughter of a Tibetan lama) appeared to be quite serious when she told how her friend had been carried away. She said it was the custom of the yeti to capture beautiful maidens from time to time and carry them up to their mountain homes. No bones were ever found, nor were the girls ever seen again. The lama reported that the girl had been carried away by a large-size yeti who answered to the common description of an ape-like being, having long, shaggy, reddish hair and an elongated pointed skull.

In an article in *Mystery* magazine, published in December 1981, Ashkenazi wrote:

> Richard Watson, a British tea planter, captured a baby female yeti back in the 1940s in Assam. He presented her to me as a pet. She was only nine months old but could speak in halting human words and phrases using a combination of English, Pushtu and Hindustani. She told me that her name was Mi Ge (Mi meaning man; Ge meaning snow in Tibetan). In many ways she was more intelligent than a human child her age. She could play 'Draughts' and 'Ludo' and enjoyed looking at coloured comics. She would laugh, smile, sing, dance or cry depending on her moods. Unfortunately she was killed by the local people sometime later as they feared she would grow into a gigantic cannibal!

Kenny MacDonald didn't take up Ashkenazi's invitation to join him the following May. In fact he decided to totally ignore him. But Ashkenazi's wild claims were getting coverage in the Indian press and eventually, in November 1982, Javed Makhdoomi, the deputy superintendent of police in Srinagar, was drawn reluctantly into the public debate.

In an article in the weekly newspaper *Current*, the policeman wrote:

> After news about Alison's mysterious disappearance had appeared in the papers, Ashkenazi wrote me a letter, published in a national newspaper, saying the police search for Alison was a futile exercise and she must have been kidnapped by some yeti, better known as the Abominable Snowman. Ashkenazi also offered to trace her with the aid of what he called divining rods. These rods, according to him, could guide their holders straight to underground caves of yetis who may have carried her away. I wrote to Ashkenazi for details and got a reply in January this year. Ashkenazi sent an 11-page thesis about yetis and also offered to trace Alison. But he wanted a price for it. It included all expenses incurred by him during search operations and a guarantee that he will receive widest possible press, TV and radio coverage. But he made no promises he would succeed. I had every reason not to take him seriously. He said he will rely on intuition while carrying out his mission. As a police officer I believe in realism not intuition.

He went on to say:

> After one year's intensive search for Alison, I cannot say Alison is alive and I do not say she is dead either. I am still looking for clues which could lead to her discovery dead or alive. Unfortunately, Alison's disappearance was reported by her friend, Elisabeth, three days after the incident. Had the matter been reported earlier we would have been able to find some clue. A special police team was constituted under me comprising crack detectives and men of the Army High Altitude Warfare School. We thoroughly combed 125 kms of Sonamarg and the surrounding hills without success. Ace police dog 'Robin' was also put on the job but no clue could be found. Alison may have fallen into the Sindh River which is generally in spate during August, making it very difficult to recover the body of the victim. She could also have encountered a wild beast which killed her. She may have become a victim of mischief. Also, Alison's father was a very responsible British customs officer and he may, during his service, have offended the Mafia. Out of vengeance some Mafioso might have kidnapped her. More than one year has passed since Alison disappeared and chances of her being traced dead or alive are remote. But I am still hopeful of solving this mystery. This is the first case I have not been able to solve in years. I will carry on as long as I live.

# 15

It was nearly mid-day when Kenny MacDonald finally escaped the cauldron that the terminal building at Delhi Airport had become in the fierce June heat and he was thankful when he reached the relative coolness of the Jampat Hotel where, by now, many of the staff knew him by name. Three months had passed since his last visit to India but this time he had no specific line of inquiry to pursue and as he killed time before the flight to Srinagar he felt empty of ideas.

> Lord, where am I going now? If it wasn't for Thee I wouldn't go, but I trust Thou will show me something one of these times. Oh, Lord, why not now?

At the airport he wondered whether the cancellation of the flight to Kashmir augured ill for this, his fifth, visit to India but he was able to get a later flight, via Amritsar, and arrived at John and Catherine Ray's by late afternoon.

The following morning, 21 June, he rose early and went to the houseboat *Haifa*. He had no particular plan of action that day so the *Haifa* was as good a place to resume his inquiries as any.

The tourists were arriving by the plane-load and Amin Chapri was away looking for business for the family's houseboats. But Kenny was able to speak to Ibrahim Chapri and the brothers' redoubtable father, neither of whom were able to provide any new information. He called also on Javed Makhdoomi at police headquarters but it was evident that the latter no longer considered the safe return of Alison as a realistic proposition and, for the first time, Kenny felt a measure of acerbity towards the man who had made the case his personal province. His army contact was equally negative. That night, as he reflected on a day in which it seemed Kashmir had closed the file on Alison MacDonald, Kenny wrote in his diary:

> Lord, I know things are black. Can we have faith in darkness? It has never been as dark as this. I must fight against my hatred of Kashmir.

Maybe it is true that Muslims were not meant to be saved. They are so spineless and rotten and conceited in a jellyfish way.

He was at his lowest ebb. His anguish had exploded in a contemptuous denial of Islam. His true feeling towards Muslims was that they were to be pitied, not despised. He had been helped, not shunned by the people of Kashmir in his search for his daughter and he had made many friends. He wanted to show them the path to Christ, not abandon them. But that night the pain of losing his beloved daughter was too much to bear.

Lord, what is going on? Will we die in this confused state. What are we supposed to learn from all this? I thought the pain would become dull but here it is sharper than ever. Lord, is this the darkest hour before the dawn? Please, please, Lord, hear us and answer in mercy. How do all these unbelievers, so right and confident in their own way, get away with it? Lord, keep us on the right road and do not let me become bitter and twisted, for I could quite easily.

Two days later Kenny returned to Sonamarg. It was the first time he had been back since he, Reta and their two boys visited the village the previous Christmas. The only snow that remained was on the mountain tops and the meadows were lush after the early summer showers. Tourists, some on their way to Ladakh, others on a day trip from Srinagar, wandered from shop to shop looking for bargains in cheap jewellery, shawls and ornaments carved from walnut. The air smelled of ponies and diesel from the army trucks that seemed to be forever thundering through in a cloud of dust.

The shopkeepers were not surprised to see Kenny MacDonald. The year before they had witnessed his unwearying efforts to find his daughter and they knew he would not give up until he had solved the mystery of her disappearance. But they had nothing new to tell him, at least nothing directly connected with Alison. However, there was one piece of information that interested him. The stall-holder from whom Alison had bought three apples the morning she went missing had, himself, disappeared. It was said that the man had gone to Calcutta to find work during the winter months. Some time later, on 29 March, he went off to send a money order for Rs5,000 to his family in Srinagar but was never seen again. Kenny assumed that if the story were true the motive was probably robbery. But it occurrred to him that the mystery may have been connected with his Alison's disappearance.

He also spoke to the manager of the Glacier Guest House and Nazir, the houseboy, but neither was able to help. Although he knew that after ten months there was little point in physically searching the area again he decided to retrace some of his steps. He climbed the steep bank above the Sindh as far as he and Reta had walked the previous autumn and stopped on the hillside to read from the prayer book he had with him at most times. It was Psalm 116 and it began: 'I love the Lord because he hears me; he listens to my prayers.' Soon it started to rain and he returned to the village to have lunch. But as it was Ramadan there was no food available and he had to go hungry. That afternoon he caught the bus back to Srinagar but instead of going to the Rays' he went to the houseboat *Sharin* where he spent the night.

Feeling very sad as I miss her tremendously, Lord, please keep her safe. Lead me to her or her to me.

Kenny MacDonald's search for Alison had taken him to many places in the part of Kashmir assigned to India after the partition with Pakistan in 1948. But he had never made any inquiries on the other side of the border. Now, with the investigation yielding few new facts, certainly none that gave him encouragement, he decided to go to the Pakistan side.

The flight to Amritsar took only 45 minutes. From there he took a Rs140 taxi ride to the border post where his passport and baggage, an army-style rucksack, were checked by Indian immigration and customs officials. Then he walked the 75 yards across no-man's-land and as he crossed a thick white line painted across the strangely silent road he knew he was in Pakistan. From his position in the queue to get through immigration control he saw a man slip something to a uniformed officer and guessed that, here, there were ways round the problem of not having a passport. When his own turn came, the only communication from the man on the other side of the desk was an approving comment to the effect that Mrs Thatcher had shown the Argies a thing or two in the Falklands. Kenny smiled and walked through.

Outside it was very hot. A taxi driver asked him where he wanted to go and he replied Lahore airport. A price of fifteen US dollars was agreed and they set off, Kenny sensing that in more ways than one he was being taken for a ride.

At Lahore he had three hours to wait for the flight to Rawalpindi and as he sat under a tree, the sweat dripping from his forehead, two teenage boys drew up in a car and started chatting to him. To them he must have looked like a middle-aged hippy and, intrigued, they invited him back to their home for a cool drink. There, as he downed another glass of iced juice, he saw that the youths, brothers, aged 18 and 19, were from a wealthy family. Their room was full of expensive hi-fi equipment and as they talked it emerged that they had been to both Britain and United States on holiday. On the walls were posters of western pop groups, reminding him of Derek and Sam's room at home in Edinburgh.

They drove him to the airport and wished him luck in his search for his daughter. Now he was alone again.

Lord, Lord, where am I going? Dost Thou lead me? I trust in Thee. I wonder if can get any sign of Alison. Lord, please bring light.

The small aircraft took off on time and the cabin staff handed out boxes containing food. But as it was Ramadan the passengers had to wait until 8 p.m. before they could eat. At Rawalpindi he took a taxi and headed into the approaching night. His destination was the area close to the border with India but he had only the vaguest idea of what to expect there and what he might do when he arrived.

He had learned that there was a school for the children of Christian missionaries at the small town of Murree, about fifty miles to the east of Rawalpindi. Murree is not far from the border and only 150 miles, as the crow flies, from Srinagar. If Alison had been abducted, perhaps by the herdsmen who inhabit the hills of north India and Pakistan, it was possible that she would have come over one of the many high mountain passes near there. It was a long shot, but one worth trying.

Kenny was glad when they reached Murree. He was still smarting from having to fork out a small fortune for the two-hour journey – £10 in sterling plus 200 Pakistan rupees. On top of that the driver insisted on playing tapes of weird music at top volume. The traffic, of which there was plenty, seemed to go at twice the speed of vehicles in India and big trucks, their lights glaring in the darkness, added to his discomfort. It was midnight when he arrived. Two young Americans, the sons of missionaries, told him that as there was no accommodation available at the school, he could spend the night at their parents' place.

> Where is it all going to end? Lord, where are Thou leading me? Have mercy on us, Lord, and deliver Alison to us. Please be with her and guide her to us. 'Call upon me in the day of trouble and I shall deliver you.'

The following morning he woke to find breakfast was ready. His hosts were an American couple, the Wilders, who had been missionaries in Pakistan for many years and their 19-year-old son, Andrew, was here on holiday from the United States where he was a student. They told him that he had chosen a good time to come because this was the weekend in which parents from all over Pakistan visited their children. He therefore had an opportunity of telling a large number of people at one sitting, as it were, about his daughter's disappearance.

That morning, for one rupee, he shared the back of a pick-up with about a dozen other people on the six-mile journey into Murree. He had gone there to arrange to have 400 photographs of Alison printed from the negative he had with him. These he would later distribute to the British, American and other missionaries presently staying at the school. He lunched with another couple, the Mitchells, and ate, for the first time, smoked wild boar, which was quite the most delicious thing he had ever tasted. That evening he and the Wilders watched a school production of *She Stoops to Conquer*. Afterwards he asked the minister if he might address the congregation for a few minutes the following morning to tell them about his daughter.

The next day Andrew Wilder went to the photographic shop to collect the prints and at the end of the service Kenny handed one to each family as they left the church. His short address from the pulpit struck a sympathetic chord with the congregation and afterwards many approached him to say they would pray for Alison's safe return.

The sheer beauty of the place, coupled with the friendship extended to him by the missionaries and their families, helped lift his spirits. He never doubted that Alison was still alive but at times he came close to despair and needed occasions like this to renew his natural stoicism. He had expected to have to spend two or three weeks travelling around northern Pakistan handing out photographs of his daughter wherever there were missionaries. Now there was no need to. As he walked back after lunch he sat for a while under the shade of a tree and reflected on his good fortune. It was the first time since returning to India that he had had something to feel cheerful about.

Monkeys scampered among the nearby trees and in the distance he could see the high mountains that flanked this small town built on a hill. Out there, somewhere, was his daughter. Of that he was certain. Although this was a hotly disputed region the terrain was too rugged to police effectively and he could see with his own eyes what several of the missionaries had told him: that anyone wanting to cross the border illegally could do so undetected. He had also been told that some of the hill tribes in this remote place moved across their traditional homelands with the seasons and were oblivious to such things as cease-fire lines and border checkpoints.

Two days later, in Islamabad, an official at the British Consulate told him about a racket in which Pakistanis and Indians were able to gain entry to the United Kingdom. There had been cases, in the past, of hippies agreeing to 'marry' Asians in return for money. All the would-be immigrant had to do then was produce his marriage certificate and wait fifteen months for the various documents to be processed. The official knew of no incidents of British girls being forced into marriage for this purpose but there was always the possibility that this is what had happened to Alison.

That night, as Kenny prepared to return home, he wrote in his diary:

> Please, Lord, let us know something soon. Deliver us from this searing uncertainty. Be with Alison and keep her safe, Lord, and let her witness for Thee, wherever she is.

Sonamarg was cut off by deep snow and for a while it seemed that Kenny MacDonald's efforts to reach the village would come to nothing. Less than two weeks earlier he and his family had celebrated Christmas at home in Edinburgh. Now, 17 months after the disappearance of Alison, he had returned to Kashmir to renew his unrelenting search.

He decided to go to Sonamarg because he knew there would be no officials there to hinder his inquiries. The local police inspector and the tourist officer had left several months earlier and only a handful of villagers remained. If the locals knew anything at all about the mystery they would be more likely to confide in him in the isolation of their own homes without the inhibiting presence of the police. That, at least, was the theory.

But how was he to get there? The bus from Srinagar went no further than Kangan and he soon realised that the only way into Sonamarg was by foot. That night he found a guide who, for Rs75 a day (about £5) agreed to make the hazardous journey with him and the next morning they set off by taxi to see how far they could go by road.

Eventually they were forced to turn back. The further they drove up the valley, the more treacherous the route became. In the heat of the day the snow had softened and they were in danger of being engulfed by an avalanche as they negotiated the steep-sided passes. It didn't take them long to realise that their only chance of getting through was to leave very early in the morning while the snow was still encrusted by the deep overnight frost.

The following morning they set off again. It was 5 a.m. and this time they shared their taxi with two other men, employed to clear snow from the roofs of tourist huts in Sonamarg. They had apparently been trying to reach the village for some time to relieve the two workers already there.

The taxi took the men to within about eight miles of Sonamarg. They started walking over the still frozen snow but progress was painfully slow and, as the sun rose ominously in the sky, they wondered how much longer the hard, icy surface could support them. After a few hours conditions underfoot had deteriorated to such an extent that exhaustion became their main fear as they struggled to make each step. The snow was perhaps fifteen to twenty feet deep. They knew this because every so often they came across telegraph poles, the tops of which only came up to their shoulders. Sometimes they hung on to the wires to keep their balance. But although they were now battling against time they were in no danger of losing their way. The telegraph poles served as useful markers and, in any case, all they had to do was follow the pass whose sides rose steeply on either side of them.

But now there was a new danger. Suddenly, without warning, the weather turned. The valley became a wind tunnel and driving snow reduced visibility almost to nil. Above them great wedges of snow hung precariously over the rock face and they feared that it wouldn't take much more than a sneeze to bring it all down on top of them.

It was a frightening experience but by that time it was safer to go on than turn back. Kenny was protected from the intense cold by several layers of warm clothes. He wore the same double skin boots that had served him well throughout his search for Alison and army style puttees he had made from canvas helped keep the lower parts of his legs dry. On his head he wore a balaclava and another piece of army apparel, camouflage netting, kept the worst of the wind from his face. They walked for nine hours without stopping, eating nothing but chocolate. But there wasn't enough heat in Kenny's mouth to melt it and he wondered whether the calorific benefit of the chocolate was being burned up in the effort to chew it.

Now, at last, they were in Sonamarg but had the effort been worth while? There were very few people in the village, which was hardly surprising. Many of the huts that had been visible during his last visits were now buried under the snow. Others had gaping holes where their roofs had been. Smoke from a few *bokharis* was swallowed by the wind and around the village the snow was studded by the tracks of animals, probably bears, searching for food.

In the tourist hut, the four men thawed out in front of a big log fire and drank sweet tea. The two snow clearers who had been in the village for over a month knew about Alison MacDonald and her father's search for her but neither was able to provide any new information. Kenny went to the army base where four signallers were holed up for the winter but none of them had been there in the summer of 1981 and

141

they were unable to tell him anything of significance. His last hope was the three or four villagers who had remained behind in the cluster of mud brick huts on the other side of the river. They all knew the Scots father who refused to give up. But although they were full of admiration for him, none was able to help.

Outside it was snowing heavily and the guide said that if it persisted they might be stranded there for three or four weeks. As he was being paid a handsome daily rate this might have seemed a perfectly acceptable way of passing the time. But Kenny had neither the time nor the financial resources to remain in the village for anything more than a day or two and rather than risk being cut off from civilisation for a month he insisted they return to Kangan right away.

The guide was flabbergasted at the idea. Not only were they physically and mentally exhausted after their nine-hour trek, there was also a real possibility they would perish in the snow if they attempted to return that night.

Kenny looked outside and saw it was still snowing heavily. Darkness was falling and he realised it would be madness to attempt to leave the village. There was no alternative but to stay put and hope that conditions would improve by morning. By nightfall all ten men in the village had gathered under the same roof. The hut was half buried by snow and access was difficult. Several roughly hewn steps in the ice led down to the door, which opened inwards, but these quickly filled up with snow and anyone wanting to leave had to dig their way out.

Inside, a log fire provided heat and the only light. The snow, which by now had almost reached roof level, acted as insulation and the wooden-floored room was warm, if somewhat smoky. There was little to eat other than bread, the chewy, flat bread common in Kashmir, which they washed down with sweet, milky tea. Afterwards each man wrapped himself up in a blanket and found a space on the floor on which to sleep.

The last thing Kenny did before he turned in was to climb outside to see if there had been any change in the weather. The snow was coming down thicker and faster than he had ever seen before. He knew that if it continued like this the guide's prediction that they would be stranded for weeks might well prove to be accurate. So he prayed. He prayed that God would recognise he had a timetable to keep. He had one other important matter to follow up during this visit to India and it was important that he leave the following day. But unless it stopped snowing, his plans would be turned upside down. That night he knew that God had got the message and in spite of the bugs in his blanket, he slept soundly.

The next morning, Kenny woke very early and started to dig his way out his snow-bound refuge. Now he knew what life must be like for the Eskimos in their igloos. A bank of snow, several feet thick, had piled up against the door and it took him the best part of twenty minutes to battle his way through. Outside the bright red sun had risen behind the mountains to the east; the sky was clear and most important of all it had stopped snowing. The top layer of snow had been frozen solid by the overnight temperature of around minus 20°C and he could walk on it without sinking to his thighs as had happened the previous day. Not only that, but the surface was smooth, as though someone had gone over it with a garden roller.

It was a moment in which he felt a great sense of inner peace. His prayer had been answered and he looked up at the cloudless sky and smiled gratefully. It was, he thought, another example of God's guiding hand in his search for his daughter.

For the trainee minister, whose powers of endurance had known no greater test than during the previous 24 hours, this was a time of great hope. The mere fact that it had stopped snowing was interpreted by him as a sign that God wanted him to continue his search for Alison and that the disappointments he had suffered in the past were part of the spiritual obstacle course that had been set for him. The memory of those few minutes, alone, outside the hut that January morning, were to stay with him forever, rather like the experience of finding young Grant Franklin's camera on the Fyrish Hill two summers before.

Now, physically and spiritually recharged, he raised his guide and together they headed down the valley towards Kangan. Another four or five feet of snow had fallen and the telegraph poles were now nowhere to be seen. But they knew the way through the pass and, on the hard, flat surface, it took them only two hours to cover the same distance that, only the day before, had taken more than four times as long.

With the Rays away on their annual holiday to Scotland, Kenny MacDonald's base in Srinagar was once again the manse where he was allowed to stay free of charge. It was the second time he had used the spartan but adequate accommodation and he was thankful for having somewhere to be alone and plot the next move in his search for his daughter.

It was now mid-January 1983 and the weather was miserable. The air was cold and dank and the streets of the city were heavy with slush and mud. And the smog from the wood stoves, which he, Reta and the two boys had encountered a year earlier, was back with a vengeance.

He had always known that if he were to find Alison it would be by a process of elimination. But now he was running out of ideas and he knew it. His remarkable journey to Sonamarg attracted a lot of press coverage. No one could deny his courage in making such a trip in the depths of winter. But what was the purpose of it? Did he really expect to uncover new information or was his real motive a subconscious desire simply to be there? The pain of losing her was as sharp as ever and often he would wake up in a cold sweat in the middle of the night calling her name. Perhaps returning to Sonamarg a few days after her 21st birthday helped lessen his grief.

If there was one tangible way in which he could progress the inquiry, it was to try to find the man who had made obscene remarks to Alison and Liz Merry when they stopped over in Jammu on the way to Kashmir. The mystery man had never been positively identified and Kenny wanted to establish whether, after buying the girls a glass of beer in Jammu, the man then followed them to Sonamarg. It seemed unlikely but, as with all detective work, each lead, no matter how insignificant, had to be followed up.

This time he flew to Jammu. With him he had the name of the man that Superintendent Javed Machdoomi had detained, and later released without being charged, for alleged pimping. The man, Ravindra X* was a taxi driver and the son of a police officer. What interested Kenny was the fact that the man the

---

*Author's note. I have withheld the man's name in order to protect his identity.

girls met in Jammu also had a father in the police force – or so he claimed.

In Jammu, Kenny went first to the home of Bishop Aziz Williams and his wife, Lilly, with whom he had stayed previously. Then, anxious not to waste any time, he set off to find Ravindra X. At the taxi rank he learned that the young Hindu was out with his cab and was not due back until much later in the day. So he asked if he might see the taxi company's records in the hope of establishing what Ravindra's movements had been on 17 August 1981 – the day Alison disappeared. If the records showed that he had driven to Sonamarg that day, or somewhere nearby, he would have some explaining to do to the police.

The staff in the taxi office were anxious to please. The log books for that year were immediately produced and an employee spoke proudly of the meticulous manner in which the company had recorded every journey made by each of its drivers. Kenny hadn't told them the purpose of his inquiry and in a moment of flippancy he wondered whether they thought he was planning to start a taxi company in Scotland and wanted to model his business on theirs. Whatever they thought, he was given full access to the documents and was able to establish that on 16 August the man had gone not to Sonamarg, but to Palgham, in the next valley. This was well off his usual beat and confirmed Kenny's view that he would have to account for his movements, not only on that day but also two weeks earlier when Alison and Liz were in Jammu.

That evening Ravindra X drove into the yard and switched off the engine of his cab. But before he had a chance to leave his vehicle, Kenny MacDonald had slipped in through the passenger door and was now sitting next to him.

"Did you meet two British girls in Jammu in August 1981?" he asked.

The man, astonished at the sudden intrusion and the abrupt manner in which the question was asked, replied that he had not. He was a young man, perhaps only 21, and he was clearly frightened. When it dawned on him why he was being interrogated he protested his innocence vehemently. He had not met the two girls in question and had never had anything to do with pornography.

145

In answer to the pimping allegation he said he had been picked up by the police because his passenger at the time happened to be a prostitute. He did not know she was a prostitute and he was certainly not a pimp. The police, he said, had realised he was not in any way involved. That was why he was never charged. With regard to his visit to Palgham in 1981, he said he could not remember the exact date but recalled that his passengers were two American women tourists.

Ravindra X said he was married with a young child. He and his family lived with his mother and he was worried what she would say if she found out her son was being questioned in connection with the disappearance of a young woman. He was deeply upset.

Kenny regarded the young man as rather naïve but he believed his story. However he made a mental note to make two further checks: after depositing his passengers in Palgham could Ravindra have continued his journey to Sonamarg and still returned to Jammu by evening? And was his version of the 'pimping' story the truth?'

No sooner had Kenny returned to the Bishop's home than the young taxi driver, his wife and mother appeared demanding to see the Scotsman who was making these wild allegations. Ravindra's mother was furious. How dare he accuse her son of such a thing. She would take him to court and sue for slander. Kenny replied that he had accused him of nothing. He simply wanted to talk to him to clear up some of the unanswered questions in his continuing search for his daughter. Finding Alison was all that mattered to him. He understood the mother's feelings but surely she could see that he had to interview her son. Now, having done so, he was satisfied he was telling the truth.

The woman was placated. She had harangued him in the Bishop's private office for almost half an hour. Like most people in Kashmir she had read about the Scots girl who disappeared in Sonamarg two summers before. It was, she said, a very sad case. When she learned her son had been questioned about the girl's disappearance she was outraged. But now she understood why it had been necessary. As a parent she would have done the same thing.

Relieved that her son was no longer implicated, the mother then told Kenny about another taxi driver, a man from Bombay, who boasted about his conquests when it came to women. Perhaps it was he who met the two girls in Jammu and invited them for a drink, she said.

The following morning Kenny telephoned the taxi office. But the taxi driver in question no longer worked for the company. He had married a local girl and returned to Bombay. Later Kenny obtained a picture of the man to take home to show Liz.

After three days in Jammu he flew back to Srinagar. Further inquiries with the police put Ravindra X entirely in the clear and now his list of possible explanations to the mystery was virtually exhausted.

He again saw Chapri and 'Cobra' but neither had anything new to say. A few days later he left for home. On his return Liz Merry confirmed that the man in the photograph was not the man she and Alison had met in Jammu.

His one remaining chance of solving the mystery had vanished.

# 16

Kenny MacDonald watched in disbelief the strange figure approaching the rendezvous point at the corner of two busy streets in Essen. The man was wearing pure white gloves that disappeared up the sleeves of a long, dark, double-breasted jacket and his black shoes were highly polished. His hair was cropped short like a skinhead's and he had a huge, black beard. He was fairly tall, just under six feet, and in spite of his eccentric appearance, he had handsome, even aristocratic, features. He looked Asian, possibly Indian, but the lightness of his skin suggested mixed blood.

From behind a pillar Kenny watched for a few minutes more. The stranger was so conspicuous that he doubted whether this was the man who, on the telephone the night before, had made elaborate arrangements to ensure their meeting would be in secret.

Eventually he approached the man. He could see he was quite young, no more than thirty, and he had piercing black eyes. In his left hand he carried a briefcase.

"Are you waiting for a Mr MacDonald?" asked Kenny.

The stranger confirmed that he was and after exchanging a few words the two men headed towards an hotel where they could talk in private.

After the heartbreak of the preceding 19 months Kenny had learned not to build up his hopes too high. But as they walked along the crowded streets of this sprawling West German city, he found it difficult to contain his excitement.

It had all started a few days earlier when he got a phone call at his home in Edinburgh from a television reporter called Harry Smith. Smith, who had been covering the Alison MacDonald story for BBC Scotland, had just received a message from the BBC's London newsroom to the effect that a man called Franz* had contacted them claiming to know where the girl was. Smith rang Franz at the number he had given in Essen

* Full name withheld to protect his identity.

and had a lengthy conversation with him. From what he was told he concluded that the highly articulate foreigner might, indeed, know something about the case and decided to inform Kenny MacDonald right away.

Smith warned Kenny that Franz's story was so fantastic that it should be viewed with a high degree of scepticism. But Kenny's experience had taught him a great deal about people and he needed no reminding about how to lay traps for those whose word he doubted.

He called Franz the same day and asked him to repeat the story he had told Harry Smith. This was that Alison had been kidnapped by military personnel and was being held captive in a remote army camp in northern Kashmir near the border with Pakistan. She was still alive and Franz's 'men' were prepared to go in and bring her out.

Kenny had long since learned to treat everyone purporting to know something of Alison's whereabouts with the utmost caution. He and Reta had once before made the mistake of believing that their informants might well be telling the truth. Now he was again being told that his daughter had been abducted by the Army but this time he was far less gullible. Over the phone he tested the extent of Franz's knowledge by deliberately feeding him misleading information about such things as the political situation in Kashmir, the positions of army posts and the geographical nature of the area.

But Franz wasn't fooled. He explained that his motives for wanting to help Kenny find his daughter were honourable. Furthermore he demonstrated a detailed knowledge of the area and it was obvious that whether or not his claims about Alison were true, his sources in Kashmir, so far as Kenny could tell, were reliable. Kenny was sufficiently intrigued to fly to Germany to meet him and now, as they looked for a suitable place in which to talk, he wondered how much importance he could attach to the word of this strange-looking man with the near-shaven head and white gloves.

The two men found an hotel and sat at a table in the far-from-full dining-room. Franz said his 'men' in Kashmir had evidence that a European girl had been abducted by the Army and was now being held in a remote army camp, high in the mountains, near the cease-fire line with Pakistan. The girl had been seen on more than one occasion and he had good reason to believe she was Alison MacDonald. Access to the area would be extremely hazardous and he wanted to know if Kenny had any means of obtaining weapons and whether he would be prepared to use them. As they talked it dawned on him that the man sitting across the table had an almost pathological hatred of the Indian Army. He had revealed enough about himself for Kenny to deduce that his 'men' were involved in the Kashmiri liberation movement and that for some reason he hadn't yet fathomed, Franz was receiving regular, and apparently accurate, reports from them.

His mind cast back to his first meeting on the houseboat *Haifa* with Amin Chapri. He, too, made wild allegations that Alison had been kidnapped by soldiers – allegations Kenny now felt were without substance. Furthermore, Chapri had also asked him about guns and it occurred to him that the real motive of these people might have been to trick him into providing western weapons for their struggle against India.

Nevertheless, he decided to go along with Franz, or at least to give that impression. He said that all that mattered to him was getting his daughter back. How he did it was of no consequence. It was important, however, that nothing was done that would jeopardise her life or cause an 'international incident' as he put it.

In perfect English, which betrayed only the merest hint of a foreign accent, Franz spelled out how he proposed to rescue Alison. He said that weapons would be used only as a last resort and that he had no intention of using them at this stage. Up to this point he had not revealed precisely where Alison was being held. But believing he now had the trust of her father he reached for his briefcase and produced several black ink maps, spreading one of them over the table. Kenny could see it was a military map showing what he thought were army posts on both sides of the border. He learned later that the maps were classified and that it was illegal for civilians to have them in their possession.

Franz pointed to an area called Gurais high in the north-west corner of Kashmir close to the border with Pakistan and said: "That is where your daughter is."

He added that with Kenny's agreement he proposed leaving for Kashmir as soon as possible. He was not interested in the reward money and if it was offered he and his men would 'spit on the ground'. All he wanted was his expenses.

The following morning the two men met again. Six hours of talks the previous evening had led to an agreement, in principle, under which Franz would go, alone, to Kashmir with a view to reaching the army base at Gurais. He would then either attempt to free Alison or lay the foundations for a bigger rescue operation at a later date. Mary McLaren at the British High Commission in Delhi would be kept informed of his progress and she would pass on any messages to Kenny in Edinburgh. If he succeeded in freeing Alison his men would bring her to Palgham where her father would be waiting for her. He, himself, would lie low in the mountains for a while.

It was apparent that Kenny was dealing with a man of considerable intelligence. He spoke precisely and economically, demonstrating an extensive vocabulary. He worked as a translator in Essen and it emerged that he had an equally good command of several other languages, quite apart from the various Kashmiri dialects he had picked up as a child. He listened with great intensity to what Kenny had to say, his mesmeric black eyes fixed immovably on their subject, and his brain seemed to be thinking two or more moves ahead. But Kenny had his doubts about him. He couldn't deny that much of what he had been told was factually correct. But how much of the scenario described to him was the product of a disturbed mind? Was it possible this seemingly brilliant man was a classic example of a schizophrenic for whom fact and fiction had been rolled into one? It was a possibility that Kenny was very much aware of as he flew back from Düsseldorf to Heathrow and then onto Edinburgh.

Two weeks after returning from Essen, the two men met again, this time at a coffee shop near Victoria Bus Station in London. It was mid-April and Franz had calculated that by now the mountain passes in Kashmir would no longer be blocked by snow. He and Kenny had spoken several times on the phone since their last meeting and had arranged to meet briefly in London prior to Franz's departure for India. Sam, now an art student in London, came with his father to see the man whose claims provided the only new development in the case since Kenny returned from his trip to Sonamarg and Jammu almost three months earlier. Kenny had with him a tent, a video recorder, a box of video tapes, £300 in cash and return air tickets from London to Delhi via Düsseldorf and Delhi to Srinagar. He had bought the tent for £99 in a shop in Edinburgh and the VCR for £199. The tapes, which included war pictures starring Jack Hawkins, were ex-hire.

All of these things had been demanded by Franz. The tent was for Alison as he spiritied her across the mountains to safety; the VCR and tapes were to bribe the soldiers in Gurais and the money was to pay for the rent of his apartment in Essen during the four to six weeks he expected to be away. The airline tickets completed the deal the two men had struck.

They talked for a while in the coffee shop and as they left Kenny shook Franz's hand and wished him luck.


Almost three months later the MacDonalds received a brief telegram from Mary McLaren at the British High Commission in Delhi. It said simply that Franz was on his way to London and that he would be arriving at Heathrow at a certain time. This was the first communication they had had since he left for Kashmir and as they went down to London to meet him they were in a state of high excitement. Kenny wondered whether after such a long absence he would bring back definite news of Alison's whereabouts; Reta thought their daughter might even be on the plane with him.

But once again their hopes were left in tatters. Franz said he and his helpers had got close to the camp but were unable to penetrate the tight security. It was almost two years since Alison disappeared but he said he was certain she was still there. Over a coffee in the terminal building, they heard his story in full. The rivers in the restricted military zones in the north of Kashmir were full of trout and he had heard that sometimes local people were granted fishing permits. He tried this and other means to enter the area legally but when all of these failed he and his colleagues took to the mountains, living rough for weeks at a time. Eventually, having got within a few kilometres of Gurais, they were forced to turn back.

Franz was gaunt and thin. He had lost a lot of weight and his appearance gave his story some credibility. But Kenny didn't believe a word of it. He wanted to show his anger but confined himself to suggesting that it was not soldiers who had kidnapped Alison, but local hillmen. He stopped short of saying what he suspected: that Franz and his associates may have had a hand in Alison's disappearance.

Franz seemed incensed at the suggestion. Thumping his fist on the table he accused Kenny of calling him a liar. It was the first time he had dropped the stiff and correct manner he had always adopted in their previous conversations. Now he was demonstrating another, more volatile, side to his character. His sense of grievance was based on the fact that he, himself, had spent his childhood among the same peasants Kenny MacDonald was now accusing of having abducted his daughter. Not only had his word been doubted, the integrity and honour of his own people had been blackened. It was too much for him and he made an extravagant display of showing how odious he considered the allegations to be.

Kenny had taunted the man deliberately. He wanted to see how he reacted to being told his theory was ludicrous in the hope that it might provide a clue about the truthfulness or otherwise of his extraordinary claims. But Reta, who had listened intently to everything that had been said, felt her husband had been unnecessarily harsh on Franz who was still brooding after his outburst. She felt that had he been a fraud, he would have never have returned to London as promised. He would simply have taken the cash and equipment and disappeared, perhaps without even setting foot in India.

The fact was that neither of them knew what to make of the fanatical and deeply circumspect character sitting opposite. His appearance suggested he had spent many weeks in the hills existing on the most meagre of diets. But whether he had actually got anywhere near Gurais, as he claimed, left more than a nagging doubt in the minds of both of them.

Their scepticism was heightened by the fact that Kenny had learned enough about the Indian Army to know that it would be virtually impossible for a soldier, or soldiers, to kidnap a female and keep her concealed at their camp for any length of time. The officers would certainly get to know of such a thing and it was inconceivable that these men, for whom Kenny had the highest regard, would be party to the serious crime of kidnapping.

From his point of view the most likely explanation for his daughter's disappearance was that she was taken by Bakarwals or Gujars, the semi-nomadic peoples who inhabit the hills of northern Kashmir in the summer months, returning every winter to the towns and cities to sell their goats and cattle. But he had not one scrap of evidence to support his theory and knew that he had to keep an open mind on all possibilities, including the fanciful claims made by Franz.

The MacDonalds had heard enough and as they prepared to return home they wondered whether they would ever see or hear of Franz again. Two days later, a phone call from a police sergeant at Heathrow airport provided the answer. Franz, who had evidently remained in London during this period, had been detained after a search of his hand baggage at the security check. He was to be charged with being in possession of an offensive weapon – an old Prussian bayonet which he claimed was a family heirloom. In the course of being questioned he told the police his reasons for being in London and the sergeant had phoned Kenny to find out whether the man's extraordinary story was true.

Kenny replied that, yes, Franz was acting on his behalf and that he had recently returned from a trip to Kashmir. But afterwards, having succeeded in persuading the police not to prosecute, he was thrown into even deeper confusion about the type of man with whom he had been dealing and why he should be in possession of a bayonet.

# 17

Kenny MacDonald knew that getting into Gurais wouldn't be easy. Border areas of Kashmir were closed to foreigners and even the locals had to have special permits to enter certain parts. He could try to slip in illegally, under the cover of darkness, but the whole area was bristling with troops and his chances of succeeding were remote. Besides, high mountains stood between Gurais and the Kashmir valley and without a guide the journey would have been virtually impossible. But go to Gurais he must and in mid-November, before the snow came, he returned to Kashmir to investigate Franz's claim that Alison was being held by soldiers of the Indian Army in this isolated village near the Pakistan border.

Several months had passed since the bayonet incident in London but the two men had kept in contact by telephone and, although highly sceptical about the army theory, Kenny decided that Franz, odd though he was, might just conceivably be telling the truth.

He left Edinburgh quietly. Only his family, a few close friends and his confidant, Professor Donald MacLeod, knew of his plans. The Scottish media's interest in the case was by now tailing off and when word eventually leaked out, it rated only a few lines in the papers and on radio. As far as Kenny was concerned, though, the less publicity the better. The purpose of the mission was to check out Franz's story and it was important that the latter was unaware of the fact. Coverage in the news media could have alerted Franz to what was going on.

When Kenny arrived in Delhi he went first to see Mary McLaren at the British High Commission where he collected the military maps of the area Franz had given her for safekeeping a few months earlier. He then flew to Srinagar and told the Rays about his plan. John Ray reckoned it was worth while trying to get a tourist permit to visit Gurais but when Kenny called at the tourist office he was told this was not possible. Next he went to see the retired army brigadier he had befriended during previous visits and the brigadier, a helpful and sympathetic man, arranged for Kenny to see a former colleague, a general, the following morning.

The meeting with the highest-ranking army officer in Kashmir proved useful. The general said he, personally, couldn't authorise a permit – that would have to come from either the Home Office or Ministry of Defence in Delhi. But he assured him that once he had a permit he would receive the Army's fullest co-operation.

The following day Kenny returned to Delhi. He had, in his possession, two letters of introduction which he hoped would help him penetrate India's bureaucracy. One had been written by a local doctor who was a personal friend of the Prime Minister, Mrs Indira Gandhi. It was addressed to the secretary of the Congress Party whom, it was hoped might have some influence at the Defence Ministry. The other letter was addressed to a personal friend of Mrs Gandhi's son, Rajiv. Its author was a prominent hotel owner who also had contacts in the Gandhi family.

On the plane to the Indian capital Kenny picked up a copy of the *Hindustan Times*. To his surprise and anger he saw that his visit to Kashmir was no longer a secret. The paper reported that the father of Alison MacDonald had returned and was shortly to enter 'a remote, sensitive area' in his search for his daughter. He couldn't be certain how the press had found out but he regretted, now, having visited the tourist office. In Delhi, he spent the best part of a week being passed from pillar to post. His letters of introduction had helped but getting past middle-ranking officials in the Civil Service proved impossible. Their response was always the same: "Come back tomorrow".

His frustration was growing daily. He could see no way through the red tape and he despaired of ever getting permission to enter the restricted area of Gurais. Increasingly his mind turned to hiring a guide and going in illegally.

On the Sunday he went to church. It was the Free Church of North India and he wondered if it was the same place Alison and Liz had worshipped in two years and four months earlier. He wasn't impressed with the service. 'Absolute rubbish,' he wrote in his diary. 'Sad to see so many people there getting nothing.'

The next day he went to the Defence Ministry, as arranged. He had been told to report to the south block at 1630 when he was assured of seeing 'the top man', the minister himself.

A labyrinth of corridors led to an office where, sitting behind a big desk, an important-looking man listened, impatiently, to Kenny's story.

"Come back on Saturday," said the minister, without even reading the letter of introduction. "I must check with the Army before we can consider your request."

This was the final straw. "I have been waiting for days for an answer," snapped Kenny. "I can't afford to waste any more time or money here. I need an answer now."

The politician, clearly used to being treated with more deference, looked surprised. "Phone me tomorrow at 3 p.m.," he said.

As he left the building Kenny felt he was being fobbed off yet again.

The next day he cancelled his return flight to Srinagar and went in search of another hotel, one where the mice and cockroaches were less noisy at night! The fifth he tried, the Plaza, seemed neither too dirty nor too expensive. 'Not bad,' he wrote. 'Boy offered me hash or Indian wife. I settled for mango juice!'

At 3 p.m., as arranged, he phoned the Ministry of Defence. "Come over straight away," was the reply. Little did the official know that the call had been made from a public phone box in the same building and that Kenny had intended to see the minister whatever happened.

In an outer office he was offered a cup of tea. This he interpreted as being a good sign, as it indeed was. After a few minutes he was shown into the minister's office to be told that his application for a permit to visit Gurais had been approved and that he should go to the Home Ofice to collect it. He had no idea why, suddenly, everyone should be more co-operative, but having at last got his permit he didn't particularly care about the reason.

> I never cease to marvel at Thy greatness – this to me was a miracle.
> No flight today, but OK as I mustn't be tired going into Gurais.
> Praise the Lord.

Four days after receiving his permit Kenny MacDonald set off for Gurais. He had been given the use of an army jeep and driver as far as Bandipur, a small town about two hours' drive from Srinagar. As they drove north past Lake Wular – said to be the largest freshwater lake in India – he wondered whether this time his long, tireless search for Alison would lead him to her. Franz was adamant she was in Gurais and had provided Kenny with a detailed lay-out of the military camps there. If the description was correct, further investigations would have to be made, this time without the knowledge and co-operation of the Army. If the description was wrong, the credibility of Franz would be reduced to nothing.

Bandipur, a town famous for its woven blankets, is at the foot of Tragbal Pass. It is also the last place of any size before the long climb over the mountains and it contains an army base. At this point the driver and jeep turned back but the camp brigadier offered a replacement vehicle for as long as required. That evening, Kenny ate in the officer's mess, and the following morning, after breakfast, he and his new driver began the hair-raising journey to Gurais. As they climbed the narrow, twisting road cut into the side of the mountain, he was glad that the jeep was open-topped. He'd have a better chance, he reckoned, of jumping clear if the vehicle slewed off towards the sheer drop only a few feet away.

Although winter was approaching, the sky was cloudless and the view breathtaking. To the east they could see the magnificent summit of Haramukh. It seemed from their position that they were looking down on it; that being so their jeep had taken them to an altitude of over 14,000 feet. The air was clear and the temperature not much more than freezing but the sun shone fiercely on the snow-clad peaks and it was difficult to imagine there being a more spectacular mountain road anywhere in the world.

Every so often they passed, and sometimes stopped at, small army outposts of five to ten men. They were now close to the cease-fire line and the presence of the military suggested that India, at least, regarded peace as anything but permanent. But as they descended into the beautiful rolling valleys known as Gurais, it became apparent that this was not an area of closely guarded military installations. At Kansalwan, the first village they stopped at, the army base was no different from those Kenny had seen elsewhere in Kashmir. He had a meal there, and noted that villagers seemed to come and go as they pleased. As far as he could tell it was a small communications base but there was little outward sign of any overt military activity.

It was the same story at the next village, Dawal. This was a bigger place than Kansalwan but, once again, there were no enclosed barracks in which someone could be held prisoner without outsiders knowing. The army commander there was expecting a visitor from Scotland and assured him of his fullest co-operation. Kenny wandered freely around the camp, speaking to officers and men of whom there appeared to be about fifty. He took photographs, even though photography in restricted areas was supposed to be prohibited and this added to the impression he was forming of Gurais: that it was far from being the border fortress he had been led to believe it was. He talked, also, to villagers and the local schoolmaster, a man from Srinagar, but no one had seen his daughter nor had they any idea where she might be. They offered him sympathy but that was all. He, in turn, handed out photographs of Alison and asked that they pay particular attention to the Gujar and Bakarwal herdsmen who spend the winter months in the valleys.

Kenny was quite sure Alison was not in Gurais. It would not have been possible, he concluded, to incarcerate a young white woman in an army camp without the whole valley knowing about it. And it was inconceivable that all the people he had spoken to were part of a huge cover-up. Furthermore, the villages he had visited bore little resemblance to the place Franz had described. There were no barracks or underground bunkers in which someone could be held prisoner indefinitely. The atmosphere seemed relaxed, or at least as relaxed as one could expect at a cease-fire line. Certainly, in his view, the army officers were above suspicion and although it was theoretically possible for non-commissioned men to hold a girl somewhere for a day or two, they would ultimately have been found out. Franz's claims, he concluded, were bogus.

# 18

Kenny MacDonald's search for his daughter would not have been possible had it not been for the generosity of many hundreds of Scots. The news of Alison's disappearance first broke on the morning of 25 August, 1981, and within three days more than £2,000 had been donated. Over the next 12 months the appeal fund was to grow to several times that sum.

Ironically, the MacDonald family had wanted little or no publicity about the case. On the day that Kenny left for India, Professor Donald MacLeod warned Reta that sooner or later the media was bound to find out and he suggested issuing a press statement that day. Reta, however, was still stunned by the news and decided to consult other members of the family some of whom felt that publicity might hinder the inquiry. It was decided, therefore, to say nothing.

As it turned out, the Hebridean Press Service in Stornoway got wind of the story the next day and by the following morning, 25 August, it was on the front pages of most Scottish newspapers. It also featured in the morning radio bulletins. No appeal had been made for money but nonetheless the cash started to pour in. It arrived both at the Free Church College, Edinburgh, and at the home in Stornoway of Donald Forsyth, Alison's brother-in-law. As Mairi's husband, he was the obvious person to take charge of the fund in Lewis and within a day or two he had set up a bank account at the local branch of the Royal Bank of Scotland. It was called the 'Miss Alison MacDonald (India) Inquiry Fund.'

The donations ranged from just a few pounds ('Enclosed is £2 towards your fund. I would like to give more but, I regret, I cannot afford to. Signed: "A Pensioner".') to sums of £100 and even £200. It seemed the whole of Lewis wanted to help. Indeed, so great had the response been that Donald decided that the fund should be administered independently and a trust was set up with two former Customs colleagues of Kenny, Donald Morrison and Douglas Daniel, as trustees.

In Edinburgh, meanwhile, money continued to arrive at Free Church College. The donations were addressed, mainly, to Professor MacLeod and came from all over Scotland and sometimes beyond. As in Lewis, the response was inter-denominational. Many of the letters were anonymous ('just a little help for your fund. We live in hope.') but wherever possible Professor MacLeod replied to thank the person for his or her generosity and concern.

A few people wrote recommending themselves or others as spiritualists or mediums, one claiming to have 'made contact' with Alison in Spain. There were letters, too, from those offering their services as private investigators. They included at least one North Sea diver and several ex-military people. In most cases they wanted the fund to meet only their expenses in India.

Letters from cranks were happily few and far between and, in any case, Professor MacLeod's role ensured that the MacDonald family was not exposed to any additional distress. He also had the job of dealing with the media, something that in the weeks immediately after Alison's disappearance occupied a great deal of his time. As one of the more progressive voices in the Free Church, an institution not known for its liberal views, he was quite used to dealing with the media and in the Alison MacDonald case he knew that newspaper, radio and television coverage was important not only to publicise the appeal fund but also to alert the authorities both in Britain and in India to the fact that the girl's father intended leaving no stone unturned until he found her. The two men were not always in total accord about how much the press should and shouldn't be told but usually Kenny bowed to his friend and teacher's greater experience of these matters.

Over the next 12 months the fund grew to a sizeable amount of money. Donations sent to Edinburgh were re-routed to Stornoway and at one point there was £6,200 in the account. This was made up largely of small sums of £5 and £10 but cheques for bigger amounts also arrived, sometimes from businesses. Kenny was also offered no-interest loans of up to £30,000 if he needed it to pay a ransom, something which at times seemed a distinct possibility.

Kenny had carte blanche approval to use the fund as he saw fit. This he did sparingly. It became clear during his first visit to Kashmir that finding his daughter might take a long time and that he might have to return there several times. Little did he know, at that stage, that over the next two years he would return on seven occasions. He therefore lived frugally, relying, often, on the hospitality of the people he met on his travels. He was also conscious of the fact that he might, suddenly, have to find a large sum of money as a reward for information about his daughter. The 24-hour deadline set by the 'three musketeers' was one such example.

Increasing the reward to Rs300,000 (£18,000) meant that, had it been claimed, he and Reta would have been forced to sell their flat in Edinburgh. Professor MacLeod believes that Free Church members throughout Scotland would not have allowed that to happen, but Kenny, who was already greatly indebted to a large number of people, was not to know that. He therefore had to be very careful with every penny he spent.

Nonetheless he knew it would cost money to secure Alison's safe return. Indeed, by July 1983, the fund was almost empty. It had paid for not only his trips to India but also the two visits by Reta who, on one occasion, brought their sons, Sam and Derek, with her. Donations had been reduced to a trickle but whenever a story about Alison appeared in the press the public responded with money and when he went to Gurais in December 1983 there was enough in the fund to support him.

After that he made no further withdrawals and when the last donation was received, in October 1984, the balance in the Miss Alison MacDonald (India) Inquiry Fund stood at £257.


My research into the Rev. Kenny MacDonald's indefatigable search for his daughter was nearing an end. Over the preceding eight months we had, together, attempted to retrace his steps by means of the diaries, maps, letters and other documents he had kept since his first, heart-breaking visit to Kashmir almost five years earlier. More than two years had gone by since his bold but fruitless journey to Gurais and he had not returned to India since. His belief that Alison was still alive appeared as strong as ever but he felt he had exhausted every possibility and that there was no point in going back until he had something new to investigate.

Several times the MacDonalds' hopes had been raised by some scrap of new information but each time their inquiries ended in disappointment. One such occasion occurred in late 1983. It was perhaps one of the most puzzling, and disconcerting, incidents in the entire affair. One afternoon Reta answered the phone at the couple's flat in Edinburgh and heard a female's voice in a language she thought might be Urdu. The quality of the line suggested the call was long distance but her frantic appeals to the woman to identify herself went unanswered. Reta said the name 'Alison' several times but the caller did not respond and she concluded that the mystery person on the other end of the line understood no English. The couple's other daugher, Mairi, was in the flat at the time and she too tried to get some sense out of the woman but without success. Then Rita remembered that John and Catherine Ray's daughter, Cathie, who happened to be staying with them, knew some Urdu. Cathie, a student nurse in Edinburgh, was called urgently to the phone but she was unable to make out what the woman was saying and shortly afterwards the line went dead. All she was able to establish was that the woman was, indeed, speaking Urdu.

Reta immediately tried to trace the call but was told by the international operator that this was not possible. There was nothing she could do and she felt deeply perturbed at the loss of what might have been important information about her daughter's disappearance. She thought, but couldn't be sure, that the caller was trying to convey a message because she repeated the same words several times. But those words would forever remain a mystery.

It was, of course, quite possible that the caller had innocently dialled the wrong number. But if that were the case why should she have talked for almost five minutes before hanging up? Reta could have been the victim of a cruel hoax but her instincts told her the call was authentic and, that being so, she was left with another unnerving question: who in India, apart from Alison and a few close friends, knew the couple's home phone number?

Another time, early in 1986, the MacDonalds received word that two Scots sisters met a girl called Alison in a restaurant in Agra in August 1981. The sisters had been travelling around India at the time and although they subsequently learned about the

163

Scots girl missing in Kashmir, it didn't occur to them that the two events may be connected. It was only when the similarities in the case were pointed out to one of them more than four years later that she got in touch with the MacDonalds. Clearly, it was not beyond the bounds of possibility that the Alison the sisters met in the restaurant was Alison MacDonald, especially since their recollection of the event revealed other similarities with the missing girl, particularly in appearance and accent.

Kenny MacDonald's next move was to find out whether any other girls called Alison had travelled in India in the summer of 1981; through a process of elimination, it might be possible to establish the identity of the girl in the restaurant. An appeal for information through the press provided the answer: he learned of five girls of that name who were in India at that time, including the one the two sisters met in Agra. For the MacDonalds, who had regarded the sighting as a significant breakthrough, it was a bitter disappointment.

However, the incident again raised the question of whether Alison might have left Sonamarg *willingly* that hot summer's day in 1981. Kenny and Reta had firmly ruled out that possibility but others, not least the local Kashmiri police, thought it quite possible that the 19-year-old student had simply turned her back on her past and gone off in search of what is sometimes mockingly called 'the meaning of life'.

It seems inconceivable that a girl from such a happy and stable background would make such a move and it has to be said that there is no evidence to suggest that she even contemplated it. Nevertheless, as a 14-year-old she wrote: 'I won't know what to do with my life unless the Lord takes me to India': so did she succumb to the transcendental temptations of the Himalayas – the land Buddhists believe to be the "home of the Gods"? Might she even have planned it this way in order to find her Nirvana?

In his study, overlooking the Cromarty Firth and with the Fyrish Hill a glance away to the west, I asked Kenny MacDonald whether this was a possibility to which he had consciously or subconsciously closed his mind?

"Alison was a solid, level-headed Christian," he replied. "She was not the sort of person who would go shooting off into the unknown because she felt light-headed. I never even thought of that. No."

164

"Never?" I asked. "Not even when you first arrived in Sonamarg?"

"No. Knowing Alison as I do, I knew this was not something she would do. I saw her diary and I also saw that she had left everything in the hotel, like her money and her Bible. She had left the room, not untidy, but as though she was going to be back in a few minutes. All of these things pointed to the fact that wherever she had gone she meant to be back very soon. Also she had arranged to go the following morning to the glacier with the Italian couple next door."

"But India is the sort of place where people from the west, particularly young people, have spiritual experiences that can cause them to act irrationally."

"I have been out there quite a few times and you are taken by the scenery and everything like that. But when you've got a solid foundation for your own faith and happy homelife and everything's going fine, I don't think you go off into mysticism like that at all."

"Is it not possible," I asked, "that her religious background was a rigid one and that in India she came into contact with other faiths and other beliefs that seemed to her less rigid?"

"Her background wasn't rigid. Her background was that she was a good pal of her parents, a very loving member of a loving family and everything she was engaged in was a good, happy, Christian experience. I don't think we should lump Christianity with a lot of other religions which are just based on emotions. Christianity is built on a solid foundation in which you are able to hang on rather than go off the deep end."

"Given that you believe she is still alive, what do you think happened to her?"

"I am absolutely convinced she is still alive and that she had been taken away against her will and that she is being held somewhere where she is unable to contact us."

"What evidence do you have for thinking that?"

"Well, it's not evidence, it's the lack of evidence to the contrary that points in this direction. I have gone out there so many times to eliminate possibilities and I've been brought to this conclusion that she is somewhere alive and that for some reason people keep her from contacting us."

"What sort of people might do this?"

"I don't know. Ordinary people, I suppose, could do it for different reasons. It could have been that they seized her for some reason that we don't know of yet, some political reason to embarrass someone else. It could be that they wanted to embarrass the Army by blaming them for the kidnapping. Or someone might genuinely have fallen in love with her at first sight and couldn't bear the thought of this white girl walking out of his life. Out there they seem to fall violently in love at the drop of a hat. In Alison's case they may have found that they went too far and that they couldn't give her back because they would be in trouble."

I suggested to him that the reward of £18,000 was a sufficiently big carrot to dangle in front of a people for whom such a sum would bring instant wealth.

He replied that there were, indeed, many poor people in Kashmir. On the other hand many had become rich through tourism and trading and to them £18,000 woud be mere "chicken feed". Such people might be unwilling to claim the money for fear of the consequences.

I then asked him about his diaries. Did he, I wondered, feel cut off from God at the beginning of his search?

"I think you'll find from the early part of my diaries that I was complaining to God that He wasn't close to me, that He wasn't receiving my prayers. I honestly felt that the heavens were brass, as the Bible puts it, whereby your prayers aren't really being answered at all. It was as if I had made up my own mind that she was dead and that God had said: 'Well if you think that, you haven't referred to me. You've gone your own way, so just continue on your own way until you come back to see what is right.' You'll find in the diaries that when I do come to the conclusion that Alison is still alive, that my prayers are opened up to God again and that I'm praying not that He's not near me, but for Alison's safe return."

"No wavering after all in your belief that she's still alive?"

"No wavering whatsoever. In fact I'm more and more certain that we have to wait on the Lord. You have times of physical tiredness, times where you have to hold yourself back because you feel such a pain in your heart, not because she is lost forever, but you are missing four years of her life. But there's never any doubt that she will be back some day."

"How would you react if Alison's body were discovered?"

"It would mean that all my thoughts were absolutely wrong and it would be quite an upheaval in my life. I'm not saying I wouldn't accept it but it would mean that I was on the wrong train of thought all this time and that I had read the signs that the Lord sent me in the wrong way. I would have to rethink everything but it wouldn't shake my faith. I would try to reassess the situation to see where I had gone wrong in my knowledge of the Lord. But at the moment, with what I know of God and what I know of the prayers of people, four years is not a long time to wait for the Lord's answer because I firmly believe that we are learning every single day and that when the Lord does bring Alison back it will be the right time and it will be to the maximum glory of Himself."

Our interview was over. As I prepared to leave he said: "One day she'll come back, so you'd better keep a chapter at the end of your book to tell everyone about that."